TESTIMONIES
OF
GOD'S LOVE

BOOK 3

Cover Design by

bespokebookcovers.com

TESTIMONIES

OF

GOD'S LOVE

BOOK 3

Del Hall and Del Hall IV

Acknowledgments

It is with the deepest love and gratitude we thank all those who contributed to this book. The willingness to share some of their sacred experiences made this book possible. These testimonies show that so much more is possible in your relationship with God. We hope that reading them will inspire you to more fully accept the Hand of God.

The authors would also like to thank all those who helped in the editing of this book. Emily and Anthony Allred, David Hughes, Kate Hall, and Lorraine Fortier. Your keen eyes and thoughtful suggestions made a huge difference in the telling of these profound stories.

"The days of any religion or path coming between me and my children are coming to an end" saith the Lord

December 29, 2013

Table of Contents

Appendix

Foreword

Are you a seeker? Did you ever wonder if there is something more? Throughout my whole life I have been a seeker. My mother shared with me the beautiful teachings of Jesus, which I still cherish and love. In third grade she also taught me the basics of scientific meditation and simple relaxation techniques, giving me a strong foundation for my journey.

I went through some very challenging experiences in my early teenage years after moving in with my father. These difficult situations gave me the desire to seek peace and love even more. I felt like there was something missing. I began in earnest to study many different teachings including the Hindu scripture the Bhagavad Gita, the Chinese scriptures Tao Te Ching, I Ching, Buddhist scriptures, and many other philosophical and religious teachings. Could I also have amazing spiritual experiences?

In college I met a Baptist minister who taught metaphysical studies. After attending classes for about a year and a half I had a lot of book knowledge but few spiritual experiences. During other points in my journey I spent a summer with the Maharishi Mahesh Yogi's right hand man, Dr. Mahapatra, and the Transcendental Meditation Movement popularized by the Beatles. Another time I traveled throughout Thailand for a month with a monk who was the head of a Buddhist temple. All these different paths, writings, and people taught me many wonderful lessons for those steps of my journey, but left me with an even greater desire and longing for more. I had reached a glass ceiling but I still was seeking something more.

In 1992 I was led to the Nature Awareness School (now Guidance for a Better Life). I had one of the most spiritually uplifting conversations of my life with Del Hall, during my first phone call to arrange for a class. While attending my first retreat, I felt a profound sense of peace, love, and excitement. While sitting in a camp shelter, Del came and sat with me. I remember feeling a deep sense of knowing that this was the true beginning of my spiritual journey. I spoke to him and said, "This is what I want to do for the rest of my life." I asked if I could return and he invited me back Christmas week.

After my visit to the retreat center I was led to a bookshelf at the massage therapy trade school

I was attending. I felt guided to pick up a book that felt right and opened to a page where a sentence that seemed to be highlighted said, "Write your dreams down." I took this as a sign from God and started a dream journal.

During my Christmas week stay on the mountain I had the most incredible dream experience! My teacher, Del Hall, came to me in a dream and helped me wake up in that dream while my physical body was still asleep in the shelter! Everything was more vivid and lucid than I've ever experienced in this world. During the dream I had a conversation with him about having out of body experiences. He then took me and we flew together into his cabin home. There I saw tables that were made out of slabs of wood. Then he pointed out a picture to me that was outlined in a glowing electric-blue light with three pictures of what I sensed to be uniquely special people, teachers or Prophets.

When I awoke I wrote the dream down, headed up to the cabin and shared this experience with Del. We spent the day talking about many spiritual topics, including seeing things from a 360-degree perspective or multiple points of view, synchronicities and signs, dreams, and the Love of God. He was able to answer many longing questions in easy and simple ways that rang with truth. I learned that as Soul, an eternal Divine spark of God, we exist beyond the flesh and can travel into many Heavenly Worlds and gain spiritual experiences.

He then invited me into his cabin home for the first time. Inside, I saw a beautiful rustic coffee table made out of a wood slab. Then Del also showed me the pictures that were exactly the same as in my out of body experience! He taught me that they were high-level spiritual teachers, Prophets, and how they can come to me in spiritual experiences, dreams, and out of body travels to share ancient wisdom and offer direct spiritual advice in how to live a better life today. He also explained how all of the spiritual Prophets of the past work together on the inner with the one who currently has the position of the Prophet.

Del also shared some wonderful spiritual exercises and how to sing HU, a love song to God. Del, the Prophet of our times, has blessed me with authentic and real teachings, both on the inner and the outer, which have had the most profound impact on my life. I have had many beyond-biblical spiritual experiences which have opened my heart to the Love of God.

I am no longer just a seeker for things I did not have. He has shined a beacon of light through all the trials and tribulations and helped me uncover the profound peace that was already deep inside. Through his teachings I am learning how to communicate and understand the unique "Language of the Divine." I can truly say that he has helped bring the Love of God into my heart and has brought me to my true spiritual home in the Heart of God!

Looking deeply within the pages of this book you may find that special key to unlock the door to a grander view of life. If you are willing to create a quiet place within your heart and contemplate upon the truths in these testimonies, then you too can discover a more personal connection with God and His Prophet. You will then experience more Divine love than ever before and may even discover your own purpose in life!

Written by Thorin Blanco

Student at Guidance for a Better Life since 1992

Introduction

Welcome to book three of our "Testimonies of God's Love" series. Within these pages are fifty true stories that show the Hand of God reaching out to His children. This book, like our other books, celebrates the many varied ways God expresses His Love. God demonstrates His Love every day, but it often goes unrecognized. It is our hope that by reading these heart-warming testimonies you will learn to more fully recognize and accept God's Love in your own life. God's Love manifests in many ways from the dramatic to the very subtle. When you consciously recognize that God loves you, it can change your life. These authors have experienced this firsthand and are now building their lives on a solid foundation of knowing God personally loves them. They wish to pay it forward by helping you to do the same. Even if you recognize Divine love in your life, it is a profound blessing for God to remind you daily of His Love for you.

One of the first spiritual truths to consider, so you may more fully understand and enjoy this book, is that you do not "have" a Soul. The truth is, you ARE Soul. You are an eternal spiritual being within a temporal physical embodiment, which is to say you are Soul that has a body. In some of these stories the authors spiritually traveled into the Heavens. They traveled not in their physical bodies but as Soul. This is much like when Saint Paul shared that he knew someone who was caught up to the third Heaven. Soul can travel free of the body while still living. When the body does come to its end, the real you, SOUL, will continue on. Once again, you do not *have* a Soul; you *are* Soul that *has* a body. This seemingly simple change in perspective is actually of monumental significance. It is one of the core spiritual truths taught and experienced at Guidance for a Better Life and reflected within the testimonies of this book. When considered, or ideally experienced for yourself, it can open doors to even greater heights of wisdom, love, and understanding.

What then is Soul? In essence, Soul is an individualized piece of the Holy Spirit. We are not God, nor will we ever become God, but in a very real sense Soul is a piece of the Voice of God, the Holy Spirit. This is the true meaning behind the statement of being created in the image of God. Soul is a piece of the Holy Spirit, individualized and personalized through lifetimes of experience.

Life is busy and full of distractions making it easy to forget we are children of God, not just physical bodies. This is one reason why God always sends mankind His ordained Prophet. We need someone who sees clearly, can gently remind us that we are Soul, and who can help us soar free as spiritual eagles. God's Prophet can teach us the "Language of the Divine," the true native tongue of Soul. Then we may recognize and understand the Divine guidance that is always available for us! Fortunately, mankind is never without a Prophet. We are never alone. This is the greatest proof of God's Love for man — a continuous unbroken chain of divinely chosen and trained Prophets sent to help show us our way home to the Heart of God. As the current Prophet my father, Del Hall III, is now in this role and has been authorized to share God's Light, Love, and truth with the world.

This book is ultimately a celebration of God's Love for Soul and the many ways He expresses His Love. It is not an attempt to place a wedge between you and another spiritual teacher; it is intended to enhance whatever spiritual path you may be on, even if that is no path at all. As you

3

may read in the Appendix, "What is the Role of God's Prophet?" you do not have to withdraw your love from a former Prophet (one who is no longer here in the physical) to benefit from being taught by the current Prophet. Having a guide who can teach you the Ways and Truths of God in both the inner spiritual worlds and also in the physical is such a blessing. Even so, if you are not comfortable accepting help from the current Prophet, there are still blessings within these pages for you. If you read this book with an open heart the testimonies within have the potential of greatly blessing you.

It is with great humility, reverence, and love that these authors share their experiences, blessings, and insights with you. They know God is truly reaching out through His Prophet to develop a more personal and loving relationship with each and every one of us. They know you too can experience even greater joy and abundance in your life by opening yourself to the truth within these pages — a truth that has the power to set you free and provide guidance for a better life.

Del Hall IV

4

Note to the Reader

All the authors who contributed to this book sing HU daily in spiritual contemplation. They tune in and raise up spiritually by singing HU, which makes them more receptive to the guidance and Love of God and God's Prophet. A basic understanding of both the role of God's Prophet and HU will help you more fully understand the "Language of the Divine" shared in this book. Please refer to the Appendix for an introductory understanding of God's historical line of Prophets and the role they serve.

HU is an ancient name for God that can be sung quietly or aloud in prayer. HU has existed since the beginning of time in one form or another and is available to all regardless of religion. It is a pure way to express your love to God and give thanks for your blessings.

Singing HU (HUUUUUU, pronounced "hue") serves as a tuning fork with Spirit that brings you into greater harmony with the Divine. We recommend singing HU a few minutes each day. This can bring love, joy, peace, and clarity, or help you rise to a higher view of a situation when upset or fearful.

1

Light of God in My Heart and Sky

❧

The Light of God is not something reserved only for spiritual giants of the past. Each and every one of us is a beloved child of God and as such, we too can experience the Light of God. It comes in many forms and ultimately is an expression of God's Love for us.

Some twenty years ago, at my very first spiritual retreat at Guidance for a Better Life, I experienced the Light of God in two wondrous ways. A lovely evening was quickly giving way to night as my teacher, Del Hall, suggested we find a comfortable spot in the woods to try a simple spiritual exercise which he had just shared with us. As the first stars began to appear in the darkening sky, I found a place in the woods that seemed just right for me. A thick summer canopy of oaks, hickory, and maples formed a high arched ceiling above me with just a very small window to the sky visible through the leaves. As I settled down on a comfortable old blanket upon the forest floor, I began to sing HU, an ancient song of love for God, which seemed brand new to me at the time. As I sang this ancient name for God I became aware of a gentle deep blue light, which appeared before me. As I kept my eyes closed and continued with the HU song I saw the light grow in both size and intensity until it nearly surrounded me. It was beautiful and serene; strong, but not blinding. I allowed it to surround me, and I felt almost as if an old friend was lovingly and gently placing a blanket or comforter around me. I knew without a doubt that this blue light was a Divine expression of love being shared with me.

Del had suggested that we sing HU for a few minutes and then ask, "Creator, please show me love." I felt that I had already been shown love before I even asked, yet I continued as my teacher suggested and whispered, "Creator, please show me love." As soon as I had done so I had a strong urge to open my eyes and look up into the forest canopy and the tiny window to the sky. As I did so, a brilliant white shooting star blasted its way across the little bit of sky which was visible to me. Awestruck, I leaned back and gazed at the little patch of sky in wonder. Of course I had seen meteors before, but this appeared at the very instant I asked to be shown God's Love, right through the center of my tiny view of the sky. I knew this was a physical expression of God's Love for me.

Later, after discussing this experience in class with Del, I began to understand that the gentle blue light I and some others had seen is rather like a calling card from the Prophet, an invitation to draw nigh to God and embark on the grandest adventure of all. And the meteor? Well, no one else in the group saw a meteor. For me the experience helped me to see there is absolutely no limit to the manner in which God can bestow light and love upon His children. And ever since then, every shooting star which I happen to see reminds me of that moment when God became more of a living reality to me, and that God loves me, just as God loves you.

Written by Timothy C. Donley

2

Meeting My Husband in a Dream

❦

Often we are given the "eyes to see" at the perfect time in our journey through life. There is no sense in losing sleep just because we did not recognize it earlier. Trust that God's timing is perfect and He knows when we are ready to accept the blessing He has to offer.

Have you ever had the experience where more is shared and understood by looking someone in the eyes than by any words exchanged? I was given a dream in which I do not recall any words being spoken, but what was said through a glance altered my life more than any other dream I have had. During a dream over ten years ago my teacher, the Prophet, introduced me to my future husband. While I had known Chris as a fellow student at Guidance for a Better Life for almost five years our conversations had remained casual, nothing more. We both had been in prior relationships and had not seen more than a friendship and a common love of the retreat center between us. In the late fall of 2004 this began to change. But it was not until a winter night in early 2005 that I was given the eyes to see what could be.

In the dream the Prophet was standing before me looking at me with so much love. He knows me so well, has known me forever, wants what is best for me, and to see me truly happy. With love in his eyes the Prophet stepped to the side and allowed me to see who stood beside him. Chris stood there with love in his eyes. At this silent introduction the Prophet brought us together in this life. I knew in that unspoken moment that we had loved each other many times before. What was shared without any words was, "Here is someone who you love and someone who loves you dearly too."

Shortly after this dream Chris and I went on our first date. This dream has become part of our history; ten years and three beautiful children later. But our story did not begin with my dream, it began many lifetimes ago. For me the dream gave me a remembrance of what once was and a premonition of what could be, all in the eyes of the Prophet and my future husband. And while I did not decide to marry him based on this one dream, it was definitely the threshold that opened my eyes to recognize him as the man I love. It was an opportunity to grow in our love for God by learning to express Divine love with each other once again.

As eternal beings, the love connections we share with our loved ones span space and time. The love that builds and grows in one lifetime leads to the next. It creates bonds of love that transcend beyond the confines of the physical world. The Divine reconnects us with those we love as a gift of love. We are given opportunities to heal past hurts and celebrate the joy of life together.

It is by the Grace of God that I was given this opportunity to be with my beloved Chris. Thank you Prophet for knowing me so well and introducing me in a dream to the man whom I have loved so many times before and whom I dearly love now. It is a gift that has made me truly happy.

Written by Molly Comfort

3

Prophet and Language
of the Divine

*Regardless of our physical race, gender, ethnicity, or
nationality, at our core we are all Soul, children of
God. God can communicate to our hearts in Soul's
true native tongue, the "Language of the Divine."
The more we begin to operate as Soul, the more
fluent we will become in recognizing, understanding,
and trusting the many ways this eternal form
of communication manifests.*

One of the truths I have learned over the
years from Del Hall is that the "Language of the
Divine" has a personal element to it. Through
this Divine language God communicates with
Soul, one's true self, and the communication is
not limited to English or whatever one's native
tongue may be. Above all else this language is a
language of the heart. By way of the Prophet,
God communicates from His Heart to our hearts.
A very short dream I was blessed to receive

eleven years ago has made this truth very tangible and clear to me. This dream occurred during a time when I was considering whether or not I wanted to carry out a comedy act in which I would play the role of a traveler passing through Russia and neighboring countries, one who was not quite sure of where he was headed.

One night God gave me a dream in which Del, the true Prophet of God, appeared to me dressed in traditional Russian clothing. He smiled and joked with me in Russian, expressing himself with great enthusiasm for what he was saying. Throughout this short dream Divine love poured out of him and into my heart. My knowledge of the Russian language is limited to only a few words and basic phrases, and in the dream I could not mentally understand a word that Del said, but none of this mattered. He spoke right to my heart and I awoke feeling filled with love and excited to follow through on this comedy act. I had no fear of making a fool of myself for I would be doing something I loved to do and knew the Prophet approved of my choice. Only the ego is afraid of making a fool of oneself. I have learned from Del that Soul, one's true self, is happy and joyful by nature. Soul has a sense of humor and is willing to try something new and different which this comedy act certainly was.

As I have reflected on this dream Prophet has revealed more layers of meaning to it. The "Language of the Divine" initially appears to be a foreign language to the seeker who first sets foot on the path that leads one home to the Heart of God. At first it may seem as hard to understand as Russian is to most English speakers, or vice versa. With patience, dedication, persistence, and the ever-present help of the Prophet, one can remember the means of true communication with God. This memory is deep within our hearts and waiting to be uncovered. Just as one does not learn a foreign language overnight, so too does it take time to truly understand and remember this Divine language, a language that my heart instinctively knows how to "speak" once my mind is no longer in the way and instead acting as a servant to my true self, Soul. I have learned not to be concerned if my mind does not always understand the Divine communication. This communication comes in many forms including night dreams, awake dreams, coincidences, scripture, and the insights that come in contemplation. I have learned, thanks to the eternal wisdom of God that Del shares with his students, to trust the communication that God gives to me in my heart. This communication often comes through the form of knowing something to be true or knowing that a certain course of action is the right one to follow; just as I awoke from the dream in which Del spoke to me in Russian, knowing that it was in my heart to follow through with my plan for the comedy show regardless of whether everyone in the audience enjoyed it. As it turned out, the audience enjoyed the comedy act a lot and I finished it with my heart more open than ever.

This dream also helped me to appreciate that God does not reserve His Love for any one culture or nationality. God loves all of His creation and can communicate with each Soul in a language that speaks to the heart of each individual. There is true freedom to be found in learning the "Language of the Divine." I invite you to begin this adventure of a lifetime.

Written by Roland Vonder Muhll

4

Protection From Car Danger

Another benefit to learning the "Language of the Divine" is being able to hear when God is trying to warn of danger. In the following story the author received multiple insights that quite possibly saved her life. They came in the form of what some would consider coincidences. The warnings were more than coincidence.

I was driving to work on a Sunday and flipping through the radio stations when I heard a voice that I recognized. It was a friend of mine on National Public Radio talking about his work. So I listened to it until I got to work.

When I left my job the radio was still on the same channel. I typically do not listen to this station but found myself listening to Car Talk with Click and Clack. A woman called in and asked about her steering wheel shaking. As I listened, I recognized that my own steering

17

wheel had been shaking for a few weeks. I was curious to hear the problem. They told her she had a tire problem and she needed to get it fixed immediately because if it fell off or broke on the highway it could be the end of her. Right as they said this my check engine light came on, another awake dream for me to pay attention.

The next day I listened to a spiritual seminar where the speaker mentioned listening to Click and Clack the day before. I was very excited to hear this about the show I "randomly" was listening to the day before! So needless to say after all these awake dreams I was paying attention. I took my car in the next day and it came back with a huge amount of problems and an estimate of around eight thousand dollars to fix. One of the problems was with my axles; they were dried out and ready to separate at any moment making driving very dangerous. With the very high estimated cost of the repairs it made more sense to just by a newer used car.

In the morning I sang HU and contemplated as to how dangerous the car was and could I drive it for a little while longer? I did not want to rush into buying another car. I prayed to God and opened a spiritual book "at random." The page I opened to talked about how life itself was the greatest blessing of all. It was a gift to be alive, gain experience, and learn more about oneself. I definitely took this as another awake dream that my car was dangerous and could potentially cost me my life. The Hand of God was guiding me and protecting me throughout this experience. I am so grateful for the teachings that have taught me how to recognize the Hand of God in my daily life.

Written by Emily Allred

5

Changed by Visit to the Freedom Temple

❦

You are so much more than your temporal earthly body. You are an immortal spiritual being created out of the Light and Love of God. You are essentially a piece of the Holy Spirit individualized by lifetimes of experience. You have freedom, spiritual power, and a capacity to give and receive love beyond your wildest imagination. You need only find the one who can help awaken you to your true self.

Having a relationship with the Prophet has changed my perspective on life. While Earth is a beautiful place to live, I have seen places where the Light of God is brighter, the Love of God seems to flow more freely, and Soul does not need a physical body to move about. In these other worlds, or Heavens, there are sacred temples where Soul can go to learn of God's Love and wisdom. Each temple has a primary teacher. These teachers of God's ways and truth were once God's chosen Prophet here on Earth during their incarnations. Interestingly, my visits to these temples have been made while my physical body sat peacefully in Virginia.

In September of 2011 I was at the Guidance for a Better Life retreat center. We sang HU softly and I began to think of things I was grateful for. Del, the Prophet of our times, explained that Rami Nuri had invited us to spiritually visit God's Holy temple called "The House of Liberation." This is a sacred Temple of God where Rami Nuri is the teacher and guardian. I was taken there by the Prophet, Del, in what seemed like an instant. The Prophet and I stood outside. The temple was tall and cylindrical with a domed roof. It was beautiful to behold and built with the finest craftsmanship. The material it was made of glowed from within like it was made of light. I had never seen anything like this.

I entered the threshold and saw others were also gathered there to listen to Rami Nuri speak. To paraphrase, he said that the way to liberation is through love in service. Give all the love that you can and in doing so you will be granted riches beyond what you can imagine. By riches he was referring to spiritual wealth. These are the treasures that truly bless and can be kept beyond the grave. Treasures like love, peace, and wisdom. This really rang true to me. To become a conduit of God's Love is not to be a martyr. As quickly as love is given to another God replenishes it.

After he had finished speaking I turned to see the Holy Book across the room. It appeared as an open book floating over a pedestal, which was also made of the same fine material as the temple. A beam of reflective light cascaded down over the living Word of God, this special Holy Book of living scripture. This light was part of what made the temple. It was alive and moved with purpose. This was unlike any light I was used to seeing on Earth. It was the Light of God! I stood before this sacred Holy Book. The Prophet held my hand. Our hands became a beautiful cup that looked like crystal but was made of light. We dipped the cup into the pages of the Holy Book which had become a pool of light. I drank the light. Prophet and I stepped into the beam of God's Light and I breathed in deeply. I experienced Divine love while standing in the beam! I had everything I needed in that moment and I felt complete. I so much wanted to bring this love back to my daily life and to other Souls who also thirst for God.

I became aware of love pouring into places in and around me. These were invisible places, as if my very atoms were getting larger and able to hold more light. I kept breathing in this light. Prophet was inches from me now. He was made of light also. Part of him melted into me. Then we came apart. Still holding my hand, he left the beam first then turned to help me. I stepped out slowly. My first step out was so grand! This moment was a special one. I was different. I saw myself as Soul, my true self. I was made of light and I was wearing a garment that flowed around me. I did not walk. I floated. A part of me deep inside was stirred in such a way that I began to cry tears of joy.

This experience is one of many incredible spiritual journeys I have made with the Prophet. This particular experience continues to bless and teach me as I relive and contemplate on the many layers of meaning it holds. I thank you Prophet for taking me to the temple. Remembrance of this experience brings me strength. It sharpens my focus, warms me with appreciation, and reminds me of the Love of God that is present in my life.

Written by Carmen Snodgrass

6

My Grandfather and the HU

The love we have for other Souls carries on beyond the end of this physical life. What a joy to know we will see them again and the love between us will still be there. In the following story a loved one, who had passed on years before, returns to comfort his grandson just when he needed it.

My grandfather was my role model growing up. He was extremely influential during my adolescent years. What may have strengthened our bond greater was that I was afforded the opportunity to share a special day once a year with him. I was born on July 7, a date that was significant to my grandfather as well, as he was also born on July 7.

During my middle school years my grandfather got sick. Even through his illness he attended all of my high school football and basketball games, and made it to many of my baseball games. He maintained his positive attitude through the chemotherapy; a fight that he ultimately lost to cancer during my high school years. My grandfather was a pastor, a husband, a father to three, and a very loving grandfather to seven, and I miss him dearly.

Years after my grandfather left this world I met the love of my life on July 10, 2012, three days after our shared birthday. I believe the two of us met by the Grace of God; her name is Michelle. As our relationship to evolved, Michelle gradually introduced me to one of the greatest gifts that could ever be bestowed to another, the HU, a love song to God. I can still remember like it was yesterday, the first time I came to the Guidance for a Better Life retreat center with Michelle and her family in August 2013. The act of singing HU was explained to me beforehand, but I had never sang out loud, rather I would sit and silently sing on the inner. When the large group of approximately fifty or so people began to sing I sang quietly and hesitantly at first. At that moment, I saw my grandfather; he was in a suit and possessed that familiar smile. He approached from the back of the room and put his hand on my right shoulder. I could feel his love and he told me, "It's okay." A sense of love rushed over me, far greater than I could ever fathom nor be able to put into words. It was such a joy to see my grandfather and I know his appearance that day was a blessing from God.

Since August 2013 I have gone to a couple of retreats at Guidance for a Better Life and have gotten more comfortable with both the HU and my spiritual journey. My spiritual journey has become one of increasing clarity and peace. Sharing a birthday with my grandfather was a blessing, but in August I also get to share another significant date with him. Unbeknownst to me, the date Michelle and I decided to marry was the same date as my grandfather's anniversary to the marriage of my grandmother, August 15.

Written by Eric Reuschling

7

Where is God's Love

To believe God's Love is everywhere can bring a
certain level of comfort to your life. Coming to know
this truth through personal experience brings that
comfort to a whole new level. It is a blessing that
changes everything for the better.

During a spiritual experience at Guidance for a Better Life I was shown where God's Love really is. As I sat in deep contemplation with the inner teacher, the Prophet, I felt Divine love surrounding and filling me. Then he took me to the earthly home where my wife and I live. I walked up the front sidewalk and saw and felt God's Love in the grass, the bricks, the steps, and the porch, like golden energy all around. Walking inside God's Love was there too, permeating the walls, floors, ceilings, and furniture. Everything was covered and filled with Divine love. Then I was taken into my car as I was driving to work. Each part of the car was coated and permeated with God's Love, as was the road, sidewalks, traffic lights, even the road signs along the way. This continued as I arrived at work where I saw and felt God's Love in the walls and fixtures. Even the people had God's Love covering and filling them, though many of them were not aware of the love.

Then, as the experience continued, I was taken back to my childhood. I saw myself as a small child playing on the floor of my family's house. God's Love saturated that scene and each scene I was shown as I was growing up. God's Love was there during the times when I was having difficulties. Then I was taken to an event in my future. I was giving a talk in front of a group that has not yet taken place in time, then a conversation with another Soul that has not yet happened as if it were happening right then. I was shown God's Love is already there, permeating every event: past, present, and future!

I am so grateful for this profound revelation. Now it is very real to me that God's Love is literally everywhere and in every moment! Remembering this as I go about my day makes a huge difference in how I feel and interact with people and gives me confidence about future events. It also gives me a deep appreciation for each event of my life. Even the ones that seemed like apparent mistakes were actually all essential parts of my spiritual unfolding, part of the Divine plan for my life that benefited me with wisdom gained and lessons learned.

The challenges of life are still here, but I see them differently now. They do not have me by the throat anymore. God's ever-present Love gives me an inner strength and sense of inner peace. With God's help, all life's challenges are Divine adventures of learning and growing in love. Thank you God for allowing me to experience the reality of your love.

Written by Paul Harvey Sandman

8

Truth Accepted Set Me Free

❦

The truth can truly set us free. But first we must be fortunate enough to be in the presence of someone adept at delivering the truth — no matter what that truth might be. Secondly we must be able to accept the truth — even if it takes time. There is no way to move beyond the things that are holding us back and grow spiritually if we cannot accept truth.

The idea of being a blessing to others captivated my heart during a winter retreat at Guidance for a Better Life in 2004. At the time I was often tense and uptight and took myself a little too seriously. I suffered from a deep insecurity that often manifested as thinking a little too highly of myself. In covering up the low opinion that was underneath I often pushed away the very love I craved; certain deep down that I was unworthy.

That weekend I was given a life-changing gift from Prophet. A healing from God delivered by Prophet is incredibly personal. It is delivered precisely and perfectly in the way that fits us best in that moment. Whether it is delivered gently or sharply does not diminish the love that accompanies it. That weekend Del spoke to me very directly. He did not sugar coat it nor soften it. He said what must have been obvious to everyone but me – that when it came to love, I was in my own way.

To the human consciousness correction can often be scary, something to avoid at the very least. It is a precious gift to have a living Prophet, a teacher who can correct mistaken concepts about love, encourage adjustments in our attitudes, and point out passions of the mind that limit not only our freedom but also our ability to give and receive love – one of Soul's main joys in life! The Bible verse about truth setting us free is very real! A correction of even a small fraction can pay huge dividends down the road of life and can be not only life altering, but occasionally life saving.

That weekend I did not hear the blessing and love that came with those words. Yet the Prophet had seen a small opening and adeptly planted a seed. Despite my inability to hear it at that time the message was still delivered. A short time after I got home from the retreat a remarkable thing occurred. That little seed began to grow and a wonderful insight blossomed. What had seemed muddled now became clear. I saw the love behind the correction. It was not done to make me feel or look bad, it was done to help free me. It was exactly the answer I needed, but I had not recognized the form it took. I falsely believed love was always supposed to come in a soft and gentle manner. Yet here I was, after a few words that were direct and to the point, happier and freer for it.

I now saw love from a new perspective. Love is like breathing. It flows in, and like a breath of air it must flow out again. In looking back with a little bit clearer perspective at how I was "breathing," it seemed to me I was making myself hyperventilate! Wasn't breathing, like giving and receiving love, often best when it is natural and relaxed – when I was not focusing on the fact I was doing it?

Del has often said that he craves the truth no matter what. The first time I heard that I was shocked. "But what if it makes you look bad?" I thought to myself. It took me years to see the wisdom in his words. It has inspired me to consciously seek and embrace truth whenever it graces my life. The experience at this retreat was a big step toward accepting more truth, not from the skeptical, vain perspective of the mind but from the mature viewpoint of Soul. Over time, with the Prophet's help, guidance, and continued correction, the healing and insight from this experience transformed my initial reluctance into an innate appreciation and desire for God's truth.

Written by Chris Comfort

9

Firefighting and the Light of God

The Light of God is real and you can experience it for yourself. This is because God still reaches out to bless His children with His Light in our times — not just in the past. The Light of God has everything you need and ultimately it is an expression of God's Love for you.

Flames thirty feet high. Water shooting out of a three-inch hose at four hundred and fifty gallons per minute. Charging into a smoke-filled building. Firefighters live for that stuff.

Tonight was a quiet evening at the firehouse. We only had a few minor calls, accompanying the EMS to a local residence for difficulty breathing. A nice calm night – the kind firefighters know is better, even if we live for action.

I had recently joined up with the local volunteer department. I was still getting to know everybody and still getting used to spending one night a week on the lumpy bunkroom mattress. Earlier in the day I decided to try something new; I brought my dream notebook with me to the firehouse. I had written my dreams down for years, but this was the first time I brought my notebook to the firehouse. Something told me I had to. That night I had an incredible dream. Del, my spiritual teacher, was sitting with me and another student. We were at Del's retreat center sitting close and facing each other.

Del began teaching and as he did a solid beam of pure yellow and white light showered down upon us. It was pure light, brighter and more real than anything in the physical world. It was almost tangible, like light you could feel and touch. It did not just shine, it went into me and through me. It cleansed me from the inside out. It was brighter than the sun but not hot. It brought peace, stability, and balance; but most of all the incredible feeling of God's Love. I awoke feeling reassured, balanced, and uplifted, but most of all loved.

The Light of God is available for us today. It is not just something to read about. God is a living God with living Prophets, and He still communicates and blesses with His Light. This dream came at a time when I was a bachelor living by myself. It showed that even though I was alone, I was not really alone. God's Love and Light were with me, everywhere, through His Prophet.

This experience was also an example of the Bible verse, "Draw nigh to God, and he will draw nigh to you." James 4:8 KJV I had drawn nigh, that is closer to God, by bringing my notebook to the firehouse. This was a tangible step to put my spiritual path first. God responded a thousand times over by blessing me with an intense and beautiful experience with His Light. I knew I had a duty to share this experience with others.

We did not do any firefighting that night. It was just a "quiet night" at the firehouse.

Written by David Hughes

10

Singing HU With My Granddaughter

❧

Man needs reminding, but Soul does not forget the sound of HU, an ancient name for God that can be sung in loving gratitude. What a joy to witness someone experience it for the first time in this life.

It was a beautiful summer day and my granddaughter and I were swinging on the swing under the poplar tree in my backyard. At the time she was twenty-one months old. She was sitting on my lap as we were swinging, just looking around the backyard and enjoying the day and that moment in time.

My heart was full of appreciation and love for the time I was spending with her. Any time with this beautiful little "gift from God" is a special gift for me. If you are a grandparent you know what it is like to hold a grandchild! I began singing HU, a love song to God, to express my appreciation. Immediately and swiftly she turned around to look at me. I knew she recognized the ancient sound of HU. Her true self, Soul, recognized this sacred sound. I asked her if she remembered the HU and she said, "Yes." I asked her if she would like to sing HU and she replied, "Yes." I started to sing HU and the sweetest voice began to sing it as well. We both sang HU for a while, expressing gratitude and love for God.

My heart, which was already full of appreciation, was opened more and filled with more gratitude and love. Sharing HU, which is so precious to me, with my granddaughter was such a joy. Her innate recognition and sweet singing of this beautiful love song has no words. We were encompassed in love.

Written by Renée Dinwiddie

11

How My Life Has Been Transformed

Your potential for spiritual growth is beyond what you can humanly comprehend. Fortunately God knows and loves you enough to always have a Prophet here on Earth to help you turn your dormant potential into a dynamic actuality. He can also ultimately help show you the way home to God.

When I was growing up I was taught that dreams were just the brain processing the day while I was asleep. I was also taught that God does not really "talk" to us anymore. When I was told He stopped that two thousand years ago I was very disappointed. Occasionally in the last two thousand years it seemed God would talk to a saint, but it was implied that saints were some kind of special people and God only talked to them, not us. The spiritual path seemed to be about making sure that you followed all the rules, if you could keep them straight, and that you did not mess up. Even then you were not sure exactly what that got you. We believed or wondered if God was there, but there was no real communication or love.

That all began to change for me in the early 1990's when two of my friends met Del Hall, who is now God's true Prophet. He had talked to my friends for a long time about God, HU, dreams, true Prophets, different Heavens, and more. When my friends came home they excitedly shared much of what they had learned with me. One thing that really stuck out to me then was the idea that dreams are actually real experiences in God's Heavens, or planes, while our bodies are asleep, not just random brain activity. It was also explained that true Prophets of God can meet with us and work with us in dreams. Something about all that struck a chord in me and I believed it and hoped it could happen to me too.

Soon after that I had a dream in which I met Del and his wife Lynne just after they had finished teaching a spiritual class. At this point I had never met Del or Lynne physically, nor had I ever even seen a picture of them or been to any kind of spiritual class or retreat yet. In the dream the students were milling around afterwards and

I was alone talking with Del and Lynne. Del recommended a book whose title I did not remember when I awoke. Then the dream ended.

I woke up astonished, immediately realizing I had just experienced what my friends had shared about. I knew it was real, and I could not believe it had happened to me. I had just met Del in a dream! I never looked at dreams the same again. Now that I knew they were real, I started trying to understand what I was being shown in them. I have had thousands of dreams since in which God's Prophet has given me help, guidance, and answers to questions and problems in all areas of my life. I have come to see dreams as an ever-present source of Divine guidance in my life to make my life better and to help me learn and grow. They have become a part of the fabric of my and my family's life. In the most special of these dreams I have felt God's profound Love for me in its purity, coming through His Prophet, touching me deeply and leaving a lasting impression. Through these dreams, with the blessings and insights they contain, God is demonstrating His Love for me. He is taking an active and personal interest in my life and is communicating with me. Wow.

That one original dream was the turning point of my life, and my life since has been completely transformed. From that moment on I became the seeker. I now knew there was something more to life that was real and incredible, and I was hungry to find out what it was. Little did I know how amazing it would be. If what Del had told my friends about dreams had been true, then the rest of what he told them must be true too. I started attending spiritual retreats at Guidance for a Better Life a few years after that original dream. Under the Prophet's very careful guidance I was given experiences with the Divine and helped to understand them and apply them to my life. Through these experiences I was given the chance to know for myself that God is real, and I am never alone no matter how it seems.

There is a huge difference between knowing and believing — it changes everything. When I was ready the Prophet took me home to God in full consciousness via spiritual travel to experience God's Love. The Prophet took me again and again until I could fully accept that God truly loved me. And then it finally sank in and I accepted the truth. GOD loves me.

On my knees before God the Father, in that profound and loving presence, I knew for sure that I was loved by God no matter what. There was great peace and fulfillment in that love. GOD loves me and will always love me, no matter what. That is the truth. It is impossible to fully explain God's Love or its impact when it is accepted. It is pure, unconditional, and unchangeable. It will never end or diminish. Nothing will ever replace it or can substitute for it. There is true security and peace beyond all description within God's Love. It gives life, joy, hope, meaning, and purpose. It can change what nothing else seems to be able to change. It transforms, heals, blesses, uplifts, and gives freedom. There is very simply nothing like it.

The Prophet also showed me my own Divine nature. I am Soul, an eternal being with a God-given Divine nature, "So God created man in his *own* image." Genesis 1:27 KJV He gave me the experience of myself as that eternal spiritual being God created, and in that experience I knew that I go on no matter what. Death is not the end nor one hundred thousand deaths; whether physical, mental, emotional, or social. That changes a lot. Many fears just drop away. I can also see that same divinity in everyone else now. You are Soul too.

The Prophet has also shown me what was in my heart. He carefully pulled aside the layers of human desires, shortcomings, fears, and insecurities I had picked up over lifetimes. I could then see a great love I have for God and a deep desire I have to be a refined instrument for God so that others may be blessed. That is the fulfillment of my existence. In serving God and being a blessing to others I have found myself, who I really am. What a gift. I have not lost anything and in fact I have gained everything. There is great peace in knowing with certainty what is truly in your heart.

The key to all of this has been the Prophet in both his inner and outer form, but mostly his inner form. Even before I knew who or what he was, he was working with me, guiding me, and blessing me and my path. He has been showing me the way home to God and giving me the experiences, including dreams, I needed to grow. He has been protecting me, especially from myself, so I could stay on the path as I desire to in my heart. He has been teaching me what my experiences mean, about the Divine principles I need to know to live a balanced and abundant life, and also about what I could aspire to spiritually. He has also healed me of many of the burdens I was carrying from this life and others, so I could walk more freely and with more joy through life. And very importantly, he has given me great comfort when I truly needed it in the face of my fears, mistakes, and apparent setbacks. God, through His Prophet, has made real a life I never knew could be possible: To know God my true Father, to know His Love, to hear His Voice daily in my heart and know it, to know His constant Presence through the comforting presence of His Prophet, to have purpose, and to live a life of being an instrument of God's Love and truth to others. I am blessed beyond all comprehension.

With the Prophet a life like this is possible for you too. Thank you God for sending your Prophet to find me. Thank you Prophet for taking me home to God. Thank you also to my two friends who helped me get started in this lifetime.

Written by Bobby Clickner

12

God's Light Shines on a Friend's Car

If someone has the "eyes to see," they will recognize when Spirit is trying to get a message through to them. This guidance can come in unlimited ways and from unlimited sources throughout your day. It might be very dramatic, but in most cases it is very subtle. Learning to become aware of these communications is an art form.

Early one morning at work I was in the staff lunch room putting my lunch in the refrigerator. My sight was drawn to a yellow light glowing in the parking lot. It was illuminated unusually bright. First, I wondered if someone left their car parking lights on but saw that the rest of the lights on the car were off, so that was not the case. Second, I noticed the sun was rising from the east over the hill and perhaps was at a perfect angle to illuminate this one light. Third, I took the scene in a bit more and noticed that the car belonged to a friend who works with me.

These three things caught my attention and caused me to wonder if there was a message in there for me. A nudge had me check in with my friend whose parked car was glowing with light.

In the course of the morning I had a chance to stop by her office, say hello, and ask how her weekend had been. As she turned to greet me it was evident from her troubled facial expression that something was concerning her. She welcomed me in and within a few moments asked if she could speak with me confidentially.

She shared about three concerns and worries she had experienced over the weekend with three different family members. She had listened to each of the individual family issues to the best of her ability but felt badly for each one and the tough times they have to go through. She could not let go of the fear, worry, and anger that was discussed over the weekend. As she shared she saw more clearly that the emotions she was wearing were not hers to wear. She realized that there was only so much she could do for her family, and the rest was their responsibility to work through, not hers. She was gaining insight into being supportive and knowing when to step back and surrender the outcome. Her willingness to share helped relieve her worries. She said she felt better, now able to face the busy day ahead at work. You could clearly see the stress that was so evident minutes before had lifted. Her facial expression now relaxed. She looked like herself again.

Reflecting on this experience I learned Divine Spirit is always communicating with me. It catches my attention in any way It can to help me be receptive to Its message. The Light of God illuminated a parking light on a friend's car at a very precise time that morning so I would see It! The Light of God shed Its understanding to a friend's heart bringing peace to her, so she could move forward with her responsibilities at work. Following my nudges and paying attention to the guidance of Divine Spirit that morning helped to strengthen my inner communication with the Holy Spirit.

Written by Ann Atwell

13

Rocking and Rolling With the Prophet

❧

Whether we are physically young or old we are capable of recognizing and being grateful for the Hand of God at work. It is a blessing and sacred responsibility to help another recognize and accept the love and guidance of God that is with them every day. It will positively affect the rest of their life.

I am eight years old, and my family loves God and has taught me about God since I was little. I would like to share two stories with you where God was part of my daily life. In the first story, God gave me the answer before I needed it. In school my teacher gave us each a quote. Mine said, "If you don't like something change it, but if you can't change it change your *attitude* about it." A couple of days later I went to a roller skating party. I could not skate or keep up with my friends. Instead of getting sad or frustrated I prayed to the Prophet for help. I kept trying to skate, and as the night went on I got better.

There was a race, and even though I came in last I had fun skating with the Prophet.

The second story I would like to share is about one of my hobbies. I love studying rocks and God knows that. My family and I took a short car trip one Saturday to a rock store that my step-dad had found on the computer. My step-dad had planned the trip for Valentine's Day. We bought some rocks and talked to the man who owned the store. He told us about a rock club that meets in our town and goes on field trips. We went to get coffee and hot chocolate right next door from the rock store. An old man "randomly" sat down next to my sister. He was very nice and had amazing blue eyes. My sister had rocks out on the counter, so he started talking to us about rocks. He told us about a spot not too far from the coffee shop where we could go to find huge pieces of quartz. We followed his directions but wondered if we would find anything. We found the huge pieces of quartz right where he said they would be! I know in my heart that it was a Valentine's Day gift from God.

Thank you God and Prophet for being with me in daily life.

Written by Cadence Boucher

14

God's Healing Warmth Brings Children

*We are loved and cherished by Our Heavenly Father.
He hears the prayers and dreams of our heart. When it
is in our best spiritual interest to bless us, with the
answer to a prayer, nothing will stop Him. Even if it
means a physical healing beyond what any doctor
could rationally explain. Thy will be done.*

When I was in my early twenties I had an ovarian cyst removed. During the course of the operation the doctor discovered some endometriosis, which helped explain why I experienced monthly discomfort, but otherwise I did not dwell on it. I just learned to live with my heavy menstrual cycle and cramping, as I had done during most of my years, and life was good.

After being married for two years a friend from Guidance for a Better Life, during a casual conversation about difficulties having children, told me about his wife having a test done to see if her fallopian tubes were open. The suggestion spoke to me and I had the same test done in the spring of 2001. I soon learned that one was open and one was closed. I was grateful for the opened fallopian tube. The endometriosis seemed to have blocked the other one.

During our special July weeklong spiritual retreat in 2001 I received a special physical hug. I believe that the Holy Spirit was working through the person who had hugged me. As I was being embraced I felt my whole insides being warmed and it spread across the inside of my belly. I felt the warmth penetrate my pelvis and surround my ovaries. I can still remember when I went to sit down on the bench in the front row, that warmth remained in me, and it remained in me for hours. I knew what had happened was no ordinary occurrence, and I recognized it as something incredible.

The next month my menstrual cycle began again. I became aware that I was bleeding a lot more than usual, and at one point I became concerned that I might be hemorrhaging. My dear friend Ann had called me and I told her what was happening. She came over and cared for me and cooked stuffed pork chops for my husband and I. She comforted and reassured me that what I was experiencing was a healing from the hug. She had witnessed it and knew about the warmth I deeply felt within me, specifically around my ovaries and womb area. She was right and the bleeding stopped. I thanked God for seeing me through and for what I received, even though I did not truly know what occurred.

In October of that same year while sitting on a bench during class and being taught by Del Hall, my teacher, I experienced that same warmth penetrating my ovaries again. I was instantly reminded of what transpired in July a few months earlier in that same classroom. A wave of warmth flooded the inside of my abdomen and went deeply into my pelvis to where my ovaries rested. As this was happening I accepted what was occurring; I was not afraid and I welcomed the loving and healing warmth that I was feeling.

On November 22, 2001, Thanksgiving Day, I became pregnant! My husband and I were blessed with a beautiful, healthy, and happy baby boy who was born on August 9, 2002! We were also blessed with another son two and a half years later! I know what I experienced was a miracle, and that my reproductive organs were healed by God. The prayer that was in my heart to become a mother was heard and answered, and by the Grace of God I was able to have a baby. The joy, grace, and mercy granted and bestowed upon us is a lasting gift. My husband and I are reminded every day of the gift of life and love that God gave us, and with that I am reminded God loves me as well. It is a blessing to have my family and I am very grateful.

Written by Moira C. Cervone

15

Simple as a Thank You Note

Gratitude is truly the secret of love. It opens our heart, which makes us receptive to the many blessings of God that surround us daily. Expressing this gratitude in our lives takes it even a step further, and fortunately there is always something to be grateful for.

One of the most profound and enduring blessings from my spiritual teacher Del Hall has been his teaching and example on gratitude. I thought I knew what gratitude was and thought I was a grateful person, but I have learned there is so much more. "Gratitude is the secret of love," and "Gratitude unexpressed is not gratitude," are the words I have heard from him, but it has taken years for me to integrate this teaching into my daily life and into my heart.

So with that learning process continuing within me, I picked up the next chart in the clinic where I work and went in to see the patient. She told me she had moved here recently but considered Texas her home. Then we discovered we had attended the same university there, she graduating in 2002 and I in 1973. I asked if she had taken any courses outside her major while there, and she replied that yes, she had taken some world literature classes that she really liked. I told her that while my major was biochemistry, my favorite professor there was in the English department, and I mentioned his name. Her eyes lit up immediately, and she said that he was also her favorite teacher.

"Have you been back for a visit?" she then asked. I replied, "No, I had not." She said that she went back a couple of years ago and saw the professor walking across campus but was too shy to approach him to say thank you. I told her she had inspired me to finally write a belated thank you from across the miles and decades that have passed since then, and I did just that. I ended my note with that phrase from Del, "Gratitude unexpressed is not gratitude." I did not expect a response, but when it came my heart was filled with joy:

"Dear James, Your letter was very touching, and I am so happy you wrote it. I am getting

close to retirement and sort of gathering my fondest memories. Teaching Ulysses back then is one of them — that first day, walking from my office to class, I kept thinking, if they only knew how much I don't know. It gives me pause, too, makes me wonder if I thanked the two teachers in graduate school who meant the most to me... And I never had the chance to thank the guy I had in high school who was the most influential because it took several years to realize the effect he caused."

So with something as simple as a thank you note, the ripple effects from an expression of gratitude can reach out and touch Souls across boundaries of time and space. I had included a sentence at the end of my thank you note, "Thank you for giving us a lifelong love of literature." I know however, my real thank you goes to the Prophet of God for giving me the tools to open my heart to a real and living gratitude for the eternal teachings.

Occasionally we hear in casual conversation the phrase, "I would be eternally grateful if..." By the Grace and Love of God flowing through the Prophet, I am beginning to realize the true nature of eternal gratitude, helping me to live life daily with an attitude of gratitude. Thank you Prophet!

Written by James Kinder

16

Visiting a Friend in a Dream

Sometimes we may be reunited spiritually with someone very shortly after they pass. Other times, it might be years later. As much as we may want to see our loved ones and friends immediately, it ultimately brings more peace to trust God's timing on these matters.

In the mid-nineties I took a job at a manufactured housing retirement community in North Carolina. My employers, Tony and his wife, owned the business. Tony was my supervisor and mentor, and I loved him dearly. He was very charismatic and had a beautiful way with people, yet he was very firm and to the point if needed. Over the years he guided me in overseeing the community. He kept me entertained with all of his wonderful stories and his delightful sense of humor. His stories were about growing up, experiences living in Chicago, and of his visits to Sicily, the "Old Country."

Over the years I noticed that something was changing. He was not as sharp as he had been and was more and more forgetful. He kept repeating things and was just not on top of things in general. I was puzzled with what was happening, and his family was having a hard time reconciling the changes. His wife took him for all sorts of tests. Eventually they realized that he was having an early onset of Alzheimer's. He was just in his early sixties.

Over the next few years his son Nick ended up being my supervisor and I appreciated his guidance. In 2003 an opportunity opened up for me to move to Charlottesville, Virginia. Then a few years ago I heard that Tony had passed on.

It has been nearly twelve years since I moved. This past week I had a wonderful dream with Tony. His son was quietly standing to his left. Tony and I were seated across from each other in a large wooden booth in an expansive room, and he was animatedly talking away like his old self. A journal was spread out in front of him, and I could see that it was full of notes. He excitedly shared about a spiritual seminar he had been to and seemed very pleased about it. I was enjoying myself immensely being with a special friend. All of a sudden it occurred to me in the dream that he was not having any difficulty conversing, not struggling for words. My first thought was that it was a total miracle that there had been a drug discovered that had reversed his Alzheimer's! Then I remembered that would not be possible as he had passed on, because as Soul he was no longer burdened with limitations of his old physical body.

My heart is full of gratitude to the Prophet for this reunion with my dear employer and friend Tony. It was a huge gift to be with him again and experience him communicating as his true self, Soul. I am grateful to know that he is continuing to grow spiritually. Love does transcend all barriers of time and space. It is so reassuring to know life continues on into other rooms of God's mansions. Thank you for this beautiful gift.

Written by Jan Reid

17

God Knows My Heart's Desire

*God knows the prayers of our heart better than we do.
Often it is only after God answers a prayer that we
become more conscious of having the prayer in the first
place. To know we are loved and that we are
heard is cause for great joy.*

Recently I was at work and really missing my family. Even though they only live thirty minutes away, we do not get to spend as much time together as I would like. On this particular day I was really missing them. I never consciously made a prayer to God on the matter, but it was something that I was thinking about and I felt it deeply in my heart.

Just a few hours later I had a break between assignments at work. I felt a nudge from the Divine to go spend some time at a local department store. Low and behold my mom had just gotten off work and was shopping there as well! The timing of this was unbelievable and there is no way it just happened by chance. I got to spend twenty minutes chatting and catching up with her before I had to get back work. This time with her was a huge blessing.

I am so grateful that God read what was in my heart and set up an opportunity to see my mom, time that I deeply treasure. The time with her was exactly what I needed that day! I was incredibly happy to get to spend the time with my mom, but I was just as excited that God heard what was in my heart and so quickly set up something He knew would really bless me and make my day! God really does love us and wants us to be happy!

Written by Sam Kempf

18

Dream House

One of the greatest blessings in life is being given
clarity about a decision we are trying to make. To be
able to move ahead and know with confidence we are
traveling in the right direction is such a blessing.
Dreams are just one way for God to comfort
us with this clarity and peace.

Last spring I was looking for a house. I found one that I was pretty sure I wanted to make an offer on but was still on the fence and having trouble making the decision. That night I asked for a dream that would help me get more clarity.

I dreamed Prophet came to see me. He is someone I know and trust. He was helping me learn to make decisions that were right for me. He sat down and I started telling him about the house. I started saying, "I don't know" about something that I was unsure of. Prophet called me on it and said I was being indecisive again. I slowed down and started to speak more clearly from my heart. Then I said that I wanted to make an offer.

As soon as I made the decision I felt so much peace and confidence. The peace and confidence remained when I woke up and all the way to closing. This dream was an answer to a prayer. I asked for a dream and I was heard. The answer was so clear and so perfect for me. I am very grateful for this dream.

Written by Jean Enzbrenner

19

Divine Guidance Followed, or Not

*The Divine showers us with love in the form of
guidance to help life run smoother. Learning how to
keep your heart open, so you can recognize this
guidance, is a core skill students learn at our retreat
center. What a blessing to come to know first-hand you
are loved and are not alone. The following is
a beautiful example of this.*

One of the beautiful gifts that I have received by being a student at Guidance for a Better Life is understanding how to recognize, listen to, and follow communication from the Divine. One time, while visiting relatives, I had an inner nudge to park the car in a different spot than usual. After being inside for a few minutes I was looking out the window in time to see a huge branch fall right in the spot where we usually park the car. This is an example of protection offered, recognized, listened to, and acted upon.

Sometimes the guidance has seemed contrary to logic. One rainy Saturday morning I had a nudge to go hang a few fliers to advertise for my daycare business. Logically I thought, who would go for a walk or go to the park on a rainy weekend? However, I followed the given nudge and hung a few fliers at the park and on a telephone pole that felt like a good spot. I was away for the weekend and when I returned I had two families contact me needing childcare. By Friday I had a new client who has come to my daycare now for almost two years. In prior times when I have had openings it has taken months to find new clients. This was clearly an example of following a nudge from Spirit in a timely manner, even though it seemed illogical.

I know that the inner communication is to bless us. I have had opportunities to learn from the times when I did not listen to or follow the communication from the Divine. A simple example was the time I had a nudge/feeling to get condensed milk from the store, which I usually do not buy. I blew off the nudge by justifying to myself that I do not cook with it, so why should I get it. The following day I was looking at a new recipe for some delicious sounding muffins that required, you guessed it, condensed milk. The nudges are to help us live a smoother, happier life.

Written by Molly Comfort

20

Just a Hug

God can work through anyone with an open heart to bring His Light and Love into the world. It can come through in countless ways — from the big to the seemingly smallest of things. Those that have been used by God to bless another know it is a joy and privilege to serve.

On a Tuesday morning after spending a three-day weekend attending a retreat at Guidance for a Better Life, I decided to go to my office early to catch up on some work. I sat at my desk before I started getting into my work and wanted to sing HU, a love song to God. It was quiet in the building and no one was around. I gave thanks to God and I began to sing HU. Afterwards I asked the Prophet (my spiritual guide on the inner) if he could help me serve someone today and be a blessing to someone. I then began to do some work at my desk and within a couple of minutes someone knocked on my door. It was a colleague and he came in.

He stood there and we began to talk about things that were work related, but he seemed agitated and bothered. We continued to talk and then he snapped at me. I asked, "What's going on, are you okay?" and he replied, "I'm fine" in an unmannerly tone. I could tell that something was bothering him, so I asked again, "Is everything all right?" All of a sudden his tone changed and he began to tell me what was happening in his life, and then he began to cry. I listened to him talk then got up from my desk and went to him and said, "It will be okay." I got a nudge to give him a hug and when I did I could feel God's Love surround us. He cried in my arms for a bit and I just held him. While he was in my arms I was asking for God's help and guidance with this situation. I told my colleague that he is loved, that God loves him, and so do a lot of other people. I assured him that everything always works out, maybe not on our time, but in God's time. I could feel him relax and release some of the tension that was inside of him. I could feel that he was relieved to hear what was being said; it was a blessing for me to hear it also. I felt in that moment that God's Love was there and palpable. He settled down and we talked some more and then we went about our day. I was grateful for that moment.

It is amazing to see that earlier that morning I had asked to be a blessing to someone and immediately I was given the opportunity to serve. God does hear our prayers, and if we ask He will respond. Maybe not in the way we think it should happen, but in His own way and time. I believe we can let God work through us if we ask and listen for His response. I was grateful for the opportunity to help a colleague by listening to him and giving him a hug, just when he needed it.

Later that week he stopped by my office and thanked me for listening to him and apologized for taking up my time. I reassured him that it was okay, and that it was a blessing for me to be reminded that God loves us!

Written by Golder O'Neill

21

Escorted to the Heavens

It is hard for some to understand or accept that they too can travel into the Heavens as Saint Paul described in 2 Corinthians 12:2. It seems impossible or even blasphemous to consider. I can assure you — it is not. Each one of us is Soul, a Divine child of God that exists because God loves us; we too are worthy of making the journey. To do so we need a teacher who knows the way.

In the Bible Saint Paul says that he knew a man that was caught up to the third Heaven. He also mentions that he did not know if it was in the body or out of the body… but he was caught up to paradise and heard inexpressible things. If you continue reading it sounds like he was actually sharing his own personal experience.

Did you ever think about the magnitude of that statement? While alive he was taken to visit Heaven. But who took him, how did he get there, and can we go? If he mentioned a third Heaven that implies there is a first and second Heaven. What if there are many more than three Heavens? What if you or I could be escorted to them to develop our relationship with God and experience just how much He loves us?

Over many years I have personally been taken by the Prophet on journeys into Heaven to experience some of the wonderful and inexpressible things that Saint Paul suggests exist. At a retreat many years ago I was among a small group of students who sat with the Prophet as he led us in a HU sing. As we sang this love song and ancient name for God, I became aware of a white beam of spiritual light that encompassed the room and all within it. This beam of light emanated from far above us, farther up than I could see with my physical eyes.

As we continued to sing HU, I had an incredible feeling of being raised up into the light. This was indescribable! As I settled in, I felt as if we were in a spiritual elevator of sorts. We would rise up and then for brief periods of time we would pause; this appeared to help us acclimate to our new surroundings. I had no idea where we were going or what to expect, but I had an open heart, a deep trust in the Prophet, and a wonderful child-like excitement.

Sometimes as we were moving up the planes of existence, or Heavens, I would catch a glimpse of color and or hear a faint Heavenly sound. From many more trips through the planes, I have seen and experienced that there are certain colors and sounds associated with each Heaven. Here are some of the major colors and sounds that I have experienced on the various planes; Physical Plane Green-Thunder, Astral Plane (first Heaven) Pink-Roar of the Sea, Causal Plane (second Heaven) Orange-Tinkling Bells, Mental Plane (third Heaven) Blue-Running Water, Etheric Plane (fourth Heaven) Purple-Buzzing of Bees, Soul Plane (fifth Heaven) Bright Yellow-Single Note of a Flute. From the sixth Heaven up to the twelfth Heaven the primary color changes from a lighter and lighter yellow to a brighter and brighter white. Some of the sounds are Wind, Humming Sound, Violins, Woodwinds, and HU.

Only a direct representative of God has the authority, the capability, the wisdom, and the discernment to escort Souls up the planes and to do so safely. As it is phrased in the Bible, we traveled "in spirit," meaning as Soul, our true self. We left our physical bodies behind and were taken to these beautiful Heavens. Our physical bodies were always protected until our safe return. As we rose up through the planes I felt lighter and lighter, less restricted, freer, more peaceful, and truly alive. As we passed through each plane it felt as if another restrictive layer of clothing had been shed. As each of these layers fell away I saw myself brighter, purer, and more beautiful. There were times when we would pause on a particular plane and Del would introduce us to a great spiritual being, guide, or temple guardian whose form radiated with a brilliant Heavenly light. During some of these journeys we were invited into a magnificent spiritual temple for a brief tour. These temples seemed to be made of and emanated an incredibly beautiful heavenly light and sound.

Each of these experiences with the light and sound changed me in some unexplained way and helped to prepare and condition me for another step on my spiritual journey. These visits, interactions, and experiences also blessed me with many insights, lessons, teachings, and practical information on how to live a more abundant and more joyful physical life here and now. Those first journeys were similar to being a tourist passing through a new city, but with each experience I have been able to remember and more fully incorporate the gifts, teachings, and love I have received. Over the years, through these and similar experiences, I have been blessed with witnessing how much God loves each of us and how much He wants to bless all His children. These blessings are not just reserved for the saints of the Bible but also for you and me. Whether it was for Saint Paul two thousand years ago or us now, there are opportunities to be consciously escorted to Heaven with a Prophet of God, and to experience God's vast and incredible Love.

Written by Jason Levinson

22

Prayer for Help and a Jump-start

When a challenge arises in life we need to do what we can to help ourselves, but it is also important to ask for God's help. It is also good to surrender how and when help will manifest. If we keep our heart open by letting the worry go, we will be more likely to "hear" when God whispers the answer to our heart.

I was excited about a visit from two elderly dental hygienist friends I had not seen in twenty years. When I found out they lived only an hour and a half from me I invited them to my home for a visit. I was thrilled when they accepted my invitation. We planned to go out to lunch at a nearby restaurant. I was filled with much love and gratitude to share many past memories of working together and pictures of friends and our families.

When it was time to go out to lunch my friends were going to follow me in their car and leave from the restaurant to go home. But the car they came in now would not start. They had borrowed the car from an older relative who had not driven it in a while. We suspected a dead battery was the problem. Normally my husband would take care of this type of problem, but he was working out of town for several weeks, so I proceeded to come up with a solution.

First, I know that I am never alone, that the inner Prophet of God is always with me spiritually. I was given a nudge by the Prophet to try and jump-start the battery. This seemed like an easy and logical solution, if it worked. As coincidence would have it, a few weeks earlier I had car battery problems of my own. I was given the opportunity by the Holy Spirit to brush up on how to jump-start a dead car battery. I had needed a new battery for my own car and was shown by the salesman how to test and jump-start a battery. I did not know at the time how useful this information would be just a few weeks later! In my haste to solve the problem I retrieved an older set of battery cables from my car, forgetting I had ordered a new set for our other vehicle and had put the new set in the garage.

As a sidebar, at this time of year a farmer in

our rural area cuts the fields for baling. It is a process that takes several days to weeks depending on the weather. The previous day the farmer had cut the field next to our property and his next step was to bale it into the large round bales of hay. You never know when he is coming to finish this task. We have never formally met and only waved at some distance to each other.

I attached my older cables to the battery of my friend's car and tried to jump-start the car. It did not work and the car engine did not even turn over. I tried several more times, making sure the connection was clean and tight. Nothing happened. My elderly friends were getting worried and wondering what to do next. In that moment I walked back into the garage and began singing HU, an ancient name for God, silently to myself and prayed a silent prayer asking the Prophet, my inner guide, for help. In my enthusiasm to fix the situation I found I could not do this on my own. In those few moments after my prayer two things happened. I remembered that I had a set of new jumper cables. I retrieved them and as I walked back out of the garage I looked down the long driveway and saw our farmer neighbor on his tractor puttering slowly down my driveway! God's timing of answering my prayer was amazing!

After introducing himself and asking if we needed help the farmer said, "I knew there was something wrong seeing two hoods of cars up and ladies standing around!" We all laughed as I said a silent "thank you" to the Prophet for hearing and answering my prayer. I was so overwhelmed with gratitude! The new jumper cables started the old car right up. We thanked the farmer for his assistance. He said he was very happy he could be of help and we all went on our ways to continue our day with so much joy and gratitude.

There are a few obvious lessons in this experience. One is that I learned to ask for help, from my heart, no matter how small the challenge. Another was to surrender the outcome and leave the "heavy lifting" up to God and His timing. I was reminded that God is constantly demonstrating His Love for us even in the smallest of tasks. I was also happy my friends and I were able to jump-start our friendship; it was a love filled gift for me. Mostly, I was reminded how much we are all loved by God and His Prophet and how much they want us to have abundant, joyful, and blessed lives!

Written by Nancy Nelson

23

Prophet Brings a Gift of Peace

❦

Every Soul is known and loved personally by God. We can each be given exactly what we need exactly when we need it. One of the greatest of God's gifts is peace, for with peace comes clarity; the clarity that allows us to hear those gentle whisperings from Spirit and the clarity to take the next step in life.

I was relaxing by the stream that flows down from the pond during a dream retreat at Guidance for a Better Life. I was enjoying quiet time with the inner Prophet and sharing the beauty of the surrounding paradise with him. The sun was warming my skin and the sky was clear and blue. The sights and sounds of nature were alive and delighting my ears and other senses.

We had been encouraged to allow Spirit to guide us to a special spot and then sit quietly while listening and remaining alert. Something that always has and always will amaze me is how Divine Spirit can be with, instruct, and bless every Soul individually as we participate together in the same retreat. We each have our own tailor-made syllabus with the Prophet. He can be with us on the inner and outer and provide whatever experiences and blessings we need to learn, heal, and grow. Anything is possible with him. I had been going through some personal challenges that were ultimately very beneficial to me, but this did bring a few rough patches as I worked through the emotions brought to the surface. On this day, as always, he knew exactly what I needed.

As we sat together in silence my attention was drawn to the wind. It was dancing through the upper branches of the tall trees creating a very distinctive sound. It drew me upwards to it, filling me with joy as it caressed my face. I closed my eyes to listen and savor the beauty of the moment. I felt myself leaving my physical body and begin to travel into the inner spiritual worlds with Prophet. We traveled with the inner sound, following it up through the Heavens to the edge of a vast spiritual ocean. I heard a gentle rain begin to fall. In my inner vision I saw golden drops coming down from the ocean to the physical, showering the area where I sat. A deep peace came upon me and settled within. This gift of Divine love enveloped me and I relaxed into it. I remained in this Heavenly place for a while longer then slowly and naturally came back into my physical body continuing to feel the love, stillness, and peace inside. I felt lighter and so appreciated this precious gift I had just received.

It is such a simple word, peace. How much do you value it? Through life experience Spirit has shown me just how important inner peace is, and I value it much more now. This peace is necessary in order to have good communication with the Prophet, to have good discernment, and to be able to make good choices. It allows me to see more clearly and to recognize the Hand of God working in my life. It enables me to have a more positive and constructive attitude toward a situation. Peace is a key to living abundantly and really enjoying the gift of life.

Prophet knows me and he knows my heart. He knew just what I needed that day. What an incredible gift it is to be loved so perfectly. He knows you too and is with you right now, waiting to love you in his Divine way. Just ask for his help and let him into your heart. I promise your life will forever be changed for the better. May his peace be with you.

Written by Lorraine Fortier

24

Healing With My Grandmother

It is such a blessing when the Prophet raises us up spiritually so we can see things clearly as they really are. He can show us the truth about ourselves, our loved ones, and others in our life. We then have more compassion and tolerance, thereby allowing us to love more freely. The truth truly does set us free.

One evening while attending a retreat at Guidance for a Better Life we sang HU as a group. Singing HU is a pure prayer to God. While singing HU and sending love to God, we had a gentle intent in our hearts for others to be blessed. Often when we stop thinking of ourselves and instead think of someone else, we end up being blessed many times over. This is exactly what happened!

While I was singing HU I saw myself as Soul. I was a beautiful, golden sphere of light. I was in a car wash with the Light of God raining down on me. God's Light was enveloping me in pink, orange, and blue light as it cleansed me. Next, I was cleansed and filled up with golden light. The color pink represents emotions and I felt that I was given the gift of an emotional healing, even though I was not yet clear on what it was. Gold light represents God's Love for me. After I was healed, I was filled with God's pure Love.

Next during this experience Del, my teacher, said that someone else could get in the spiritual shower with us. I saw my grandmother with me and we were both surrounded by white light. During this experience my grandmother looked so free, weightless, and excited in a childlike way. Her face was relaxed and lit up with happiness. In the physical my grandmother can be grumpy and difficult to get along with at times. During this experience I was able to witness Grandma as her true self, Soul. I was grateful to see this more real side of my grandmother instead of the rough exterior I see sometimes in the physical.

When I shared this experience in class it was pointed out to me that maybe my grandmother has a rough exterior to cover up fear, pain, and loneliness deep down. My grandmother was married two times and both of her husbands died of cancer. Grandma definitely misses them and I know she is lonely. Del pointed out many feelings that my grandmother may be experiencing that could cause her to not be the most pleasant person to be around. I had not considered this side before. This experience, by the Grace of God, has shown me a new way to view my grandmother. Instead of seeing just the outer, I have more clarity and empathy towards her. This has freed me from my own judgments and I am able to love Grandma more freely and on a deeper level.

This experience has not only shown me a different way to see my grandmother but also understand that other people I come across in life may be going through difficult times, which could cause them to act more prickly towards others. After this experience I have been able to change my perspective and attitudes towards a few people in my life, as well as strangers I come across in stores, on the phone, at work, etc. I found that by not judging people based on their surface waves I am more free to treat them how I would like for them to treat me. It is easier to give solace and have compassion for others when I see them as Soul. Not only is this a gift for others, but it also allows me to live more freely.

Thank you Prophet for this valuable experience.

Written by Michelle K. Reuschling

25

A Wave of God's Love

Each and every one of us can be a point of light in our respective spheres. Our friends, family, and the countless others whose paths we cross in the course of our day can be lifted up in our presence. It is a conscious choice on our part to stay tuned in with Spirit and allow the Love of God to flow through us - wherever we are. What a wonderful way to serve.

Several years ago I stood in line at the grocery store. The store was so crowded that even the line for the Express Lane went halfway down an aisle. As I waited I silently sang HU, that glorious love song to God, as taught to me by Del Hall, my teacher and a true Prophet of God. As the line crawled forward a large man got in line directly behind me. He seemed quite agitated. He complained rather loudly about the long line, slamming his keys repeatedly against a shelf. I felt uncomfortable standing next to him. Others in line seemed to be trying to pretend he or they were somewhere else. His intensity was building and it seemed like sooner or later someone was going to be on the receiving end of his apparent frustration. I was pretty sure the clerk running the cash register in our lane was going to be that someone.

The line shuffled along awkwardly for several more minutes until finally I reached the conveyor belt near the register. The man behind me said, "Excuse me," abruptly shoving his items down next to me. He grumbled again about having to wait so long. If you've ever worked in retail or worked a cash register you know that a single individual can sometimes greatly affect your day, especially when you are tired. You might see a hundred people in a day, but one single customer can stand out as being exceptionally kind or unpleasant. Prophet has taught for years that we affect others with our words, thoughts, and actions. We cannot control whether or not we send out waves of energy that impact others (either negatively or positively), but we do have control over what kind of energy we send out. "What kind of waves do you want to make?" Del would often ask us.

I had managed to keep my heart open and continued to sing HU silently in the checkout line when I got the nudge to speak to the man. With a deep breath and silent trust in the Prophet I turned and said, "Not very fast today, are they?" - stating the incredibly obvious. Instead of agitating him further, my words instead seemed to calm him. He agreed with my obvious statement and added that it is never fast. The Express Lane is *always* slow in every grocery store he goes into. I made another agreeable comment and then a weird thing happened. We both laughed. It was like Spirit turned a release valve and let off a great deal of pressure. It was very tangible.

I turned back in line and after a few more moments finally reached the cashier. I turned to him again and jokingly said, "End of the line, finally, you almost made it!" He chuckled and said, "Yeah, NOW it's the Express Lane!" When I finished paying he said, "You take care now." I looked back and smiled as I heard the cashier ask him, "How are you today?" The man calmly responded, "I'm doing okay, thank you."

Spirit will not violate one's free will, and it was not my intention to change the man's mind or mood. Singing HU kept my heart open to God, and the Holy Spirit found an opening to gracefully diffuse an uncomfortable situation. I was blessed to see the Hand of God grace my everyday life. Perhaps the man was blessed to cast some of his cares behind and have a better day, and the cashier was spared from a potentially unpleasant interaction.

Life is full of situations like that; seemingly small and commonplace experiences that challenge and test us. These experiences offer the opportunity to be a victim of circumstances or remain above the fray. Being aware of the Prophet spiritually as we go about our day can inspire us to be more of the cause in our lives and less the effect of others' moods, words, and opinions. How freeing this is to experience! God loves us and wants us to be happy! How incredibly blessed I am to know a living Prophet who teaches me to do this very thing. What kind of waves do you want to send out?

Written by Chris Comfort

26

Lonely No More

Even during the times when there is no one else in your life physically, if you focus on gratitude it can ease the loneliness. Gratitude for your blessings opens your heart and helps you to recognize God's loving Presence. This presence is ALWAYS there whether you feel it or not. When you recognize in a very real sense that you are never alone, joy will follow.

I am single now for the first time in many years. I came home from work one day and was struck by an intense loneliness. I realized fairly quickly that I was focusing on it and decided to change that. Life is given to us by God moment to moment. I sang HU, a love song to God. It is a pure prayer saying "Thank you, I Love you." What better way to start living in the moment.

I got up afterwards and opened my drapes. It was raining outside so I grabbed a chair and sat under my covered porch. I breathed in the damp air, listening to the sound of the rain on the deck above and in the leaves on the trees. The colors of the woods around me were vibrant in the rain, seeming especially alive.

My eyes were drawn to my grill and I smiled. I had a roast thawed out and really savored it slow-cooked, joined by a red potato and broccoli smothered in butter. I looked around my apartment as I cooked, really appreciating where I lived, paying attention to details that I do not usually notice because it's there everyday. I was not focusing on my usual to-do list, but just being aware of the moment and where I was.

I had a nudge, a gentle touch by the Divine, to write the experience down and share it. As I did I realized I had not been lonely for hours, and why would I be? I was living in the moment with the blessings of God all around me, strongly feeling and experiencing the presence of my inner guide the whole time. I even remembered a movie from the night before that spoke about living in the moment. I am so loved by God that I was given a heads up and I was glad I listened.

I shared this story with a friend who wisely said, "Loneliness is focusing on what you don't have." It is so true. I am reminded to live my life with purpose, every moment a gift of love from a living God. Thank You!   Written by Gary Caudle

27

A Letter of Healing

When we close our hearts in an attempt to avoid pain in one area of our life it ends up limiting the amount of love we can give and receive in all areas of our life. No matter the reason, if our heart is open — it's open, if our heart is closed — it's closed. It is a package deal. Thank God the Prophet knows this and can gently help us to heal all areas of our life.

This is my experience of the beginning of the healing between my father and me. Little did I know at the time that it was the beginning of so much more. My father's and my relationship had been strained and stressful since a very early age of my life. My father had some mental health challenges and our family life and environment was volatile much of the time. I knew my dad loved me, but the way I responded and reacted to him and most situations was to close down.

I was attending a weeklong retreat taught by Del, the Prophet. Del suggested to the class to write a letter of love and appreciation to someone as a healing exercise. At that time of my life I had been avoiding any contact with my father even though he would sometimes reach out to me.

I started to sing HU, a love song to God, to try to open my heart toward my father. I also asked Prophet on the inner for help in writing my letter. After singing HU and with Prophet's help I was able to open my heart and think of my dad in a new and more truthful way. I was gifted with recognition of the love he had for me and the ways he had shown that love through the years. I was now open to expressing appreciation and acknowledging the things he had done for me. Things that before this exercise I was never able to express to him or even myself. I also was able to apologize for my actions that I knew had caused him sorrow and pain and that I also held guilt about.

Del told us we did not have to mail the letter, but I did. It was the first time I had lovingly reached out to my dad in many years. It seemed on the surface to be a simple exercise, but it had a deep and healing effect on me and my father. Over time I began to realize just how deep. By writing this letter with the Prophet there was a healing in me. I softened and my heart opened more. Before this letter I had thought that by closing my heart I was keeping out the pain, but actually I was limiting the amount of love I could give and receive in ALL areas of my life. On one level this was a simple exercise, but through the Prophet, the Hand of God was involved in this experience and it was profound. Del as the Prophet of God is authorized to speak for God, so when this exercise was suggested God was involved.

My dad told me he received the letter and appreciated it, resulting in a beautiful change in our relationship. One might think it was because of the outer letter, and some of it was. However, most of the healing came from deep within which only God can do. The change that occurred was not only in my relationship with my father; the blessings of this healing also changed my relationship with my children, husband, friends, and the way I relate in life. I am so appreciative of my relationship with the Prophet; the ripples from that healing continue to affect all those that I come in contact with.

Written by Renée Dinwiddie

28

Never Give Up on Love

Many marriages fail even when there is true love between the two Souls. For love to be of actual value it must be expressed and accepted, which becomes more and more difficult when our hearts are closed. When each partner is "right with God" and acts on His guidance, a marriage will truly flourish.

Having a beautiful life and enjoying it are two different things. Even a little lack of peace in one key area of our lives can create a wedge between us and true happiness. It can start to crowd out the joy and the love that is there by the Grace of God. My marriage produced three beautiful children in a wonderful home surrounded by family, friends, and loved ones, but issues between my wife and I always seemed to get in the way of a stable foundation. Despite the blessings and abundance that God poured over our lives we were closer to getting a divorce than reaching our tenth anniversary. The love was there between us, but it never seemed to find its way. A wall of words; often harsh, bitter, and angry, expressed our growing frustration and unhappiness.

We tried counseling, worked on our communication, read books, listened to tapes, wrote down our goals together, but no lasting change came of it. We never could seem to clean the slate of the issues that plagued us. We had gone around and around in circles spinning our wheels until we were both worn out. It was affecting every area of our lives. A big part of this dream life was dying and I felt helpless to do anything about it. In a place of resignation I arrived at Guidance for a Better Life in November of last year for a weekend retreat. My heart was heavy. I was out of ideas, patience, and motivation. I was not happy with the results I was getting, and though I could not admit it at the time, I was very unhappy with myself. Something had to change.

There is a plus factor being in the physical presence of Del, my teacher, a true Prophet of God. Though communication extends beyond the physical, being there in person has its benefits. From the time I stepped onto the property I began to relax. In my experience, it is much harder to hear Spirit when we are uptight.

We keep asking and keep praying with more volume and intensity and wonder why God does not answer us. Sometimes stepping back to take a deep breath and actually listen, with our ears *and* our heart, makes all the difference.

Within an hour of being on the property I was given an inner insight to a simple exercise to try when I went home. No words were spoken outwardly, but the Prophet, adept at reading hearts, spoke directly to mine. The suggestion? Bring a simple dry erase board to my wife and begin to write down all the issues in our marriage and all those things she and I wished and prayed to be gone from our marriage; erasing each one, multiple times if necessary, until it was fully erased from our hearts and lives. Then on the other side of the board we were to fill it with those qualities we truly wanted to manifest, writing each one down as a foundation of our renewed covenant.

I felt hope well up in my heart for the first time in awhile. If my wife was willing to try it there just might be a chance it could work. The retreat could have ended at this point and I would have been content, but my heart was still not conditioned to accept the healing I was being offered by the Divine. There were two more crucial components that were needed before I went home to share my gift. First, I was given the gift of remembrance. During an inner contemplation the Prophet took me back over every year of my marriage. With incredible clarity and detail I was able to view my actions and regrets with kindness and understanding. Rising above the harsh emotional and critical viewpoint I was able to forgive *myself*, something that proved far harder than forgiving my wife.

The second gift was delivered when I sang HU together with the group. During the sacred love song to God, the space in my heart that was opened by forgiving myself was filled with such a deep peace that I committed never to let anything ever again steal it away. My heart was now ready. With my priorities put back in their proper order – God first, then my marriage – I felt confident all would work out for the best. When I arrived home my excitement to share this gift from God trumped any worries or concerns. I explained what I wanted to try and then wrote down a couple of issues I was ready to let go of on the board. When I finally wrote down something I knew my wife would be thrilled to see gone, I watched her initial reluctance disappear. She then joined me in naming and then surrendering, one by one, the hurt and pain.

The results were stunning; greater than I could have hoped for. Every issue written down and erased seemed to lift almost immediately, like the Hands of God scooped it off our shoulders and out of our lives. These were things we had spent hours and weeks and years "discussing" to no avail. Yet they seemed to melt away almost before we had written them on the board to erase them. For several hours that night, and for the next several days, we continued to write down these things slowly weeding them out of our lives. We had both prayed and tried and now, in God's timing and Grace, they were being removed.

Later in the week when we finally felt there was some room in our marriage and in our hearts again, we turned the board over for the second part of the exercise. We began adding the things we wanted to cultivate in our marriage: to help one another become the best we can be spiritually, to be a harbor of love, and to demonstrate our love and respect on a daily basis. It was as if the Hands of God were filling us up with these Divine qualities. Months later our relationship, rich and full with the fruit of the

Spirit, is now also enjoyable, engaging, and fun. It is not only a better relationship, it is a transformed one.

God gave me a simple suggestion to follow through His Prophet, Del Hall. Following that advice in a timely manner has made all the difference in the world. It was the missing "peace" and the breakthrough we had been praying for. How grateful I am God heard and answered my prayer. The positive ripples from this simple gift will be felt for generations to come. This tool works in other areas of life, not just in relationships. Our ability to make conscious choices in our lives – to choose what we want to nurture and what we want to eliminate – is one of God's sublime gifts to us. Is there an area in your life you would like to welcome the Hand of God to transform?

Written by Chris Comfort

29

Skills to Cope With Depression

We all face challenges in life, which are ultimately opportunities for growth. During these times we can actually forge a deeper relationship and appreciation for God. One key is to not lose sight of the Hand of God that is available. Those that ask God for help and also do their part will ultimately come out stronger, versus just "make it through."

About two years ago my life changed. Everyone goes through changes, but this was one of those major turning points for me. I had recently moved with my husband and two young children to a town where we did not know anyone. The move required that I leave a job I really liked and enjoyed. Then we had our third child. To me this was a whole lot of change in a very short period of time.

I thought I had prepared for these changes. I am not complaining, I have a very good and happy life. I knew all these changes were blessings, but I was struggling. I was experiencing some level of baby blues or postpartum depression, and all the changes added to how I was feeling. This concerned me because I knew depression. I had been depressed at earlier times in my life and did not want to go there again.

Between my personal history and experience from my previous job I had some tools and skills to manage this issue. In the past I did my best to just "make it through" those tough times, but this time was different because I knew that the Hand of God was working in my life. I have been blessed to experience God's Love in so many ways. Over the years I have built a loving and trusting relationship with God's Prophet, the Hand of God. So when I recognized my situation I now knew how to more than just "make it through." This time I knew I had help available. I asked for help and accepted that help. I listened and followed the Divine guidance given to me with love and compassion. I knew his comfort. I knew that even in the moments when I felt alone that I am never alone. The Prophet is with me every moment. He helped me have the strength to do my part; to wisely use the tools and skills I had been taught in the past, and to truly know I could do it with him. So this time my experience with depression really was different and I am forever grateful.

I kept praying for help and continued attending retreats at Guidance for a Better Life. That is where I originally learned about God's Prophet and the importance of our relationship. Everything continued to build toward a good outcome. The inner guide, inner Prophet, and I spent time in scripture, reading spiritual books, putting love into everything that we did throughout the day, and being grateful. Together we sang HU with and to my baby even in those tired, weary, early weeks and so much more. I paid attention to my dreams and used those late night feedings awake with the baby as an opportunity to write them down and say, "Thank you." The Prophet nudged me to speak up for myself and take care of myself. He encouraged me to step out of my comfort zone and join activities and social groups where I met wonderful, welcoming people in the community.

God responded by guiding and helping me daily. Life was enjoyable and not a struggle. I had faith in Him and in turn He helped me have faith in myself to keep going forward. I came out better than ever and feel I have a stronger and deeper relationship with the Prophet than I even had before. My life was good, but now I was appreciating it more. My sacred relationship with the Prophet makes my life abundant and it is continually growing.

Instead of spiraling down and retreating into depression like I had in the past, I stepped out, survived, and then thrived with my focus on God's Love. Things were not distorted as they had been before in that same space and frame of mind because the Prophet helped me to see clearly from a higher view, as Soul. That higher view helped me to appreciate the gifts of God that were everywhere around me. My heart was open and filled with love, which gave me the opportunity to enjoy loving and caring for my family again. I allowed love in, so I could give it out to others, and was shown a deeper understanding of giving and receiving love. I am very thankful for the blessing to walk with the Prophet daily and to give and receive God's Love. It has changed my life.

Written by Michelle Hibshman

30

Green Light of God and the Abundant Life

Withdrawing from the physical temporal world and its distractions to sit and contemplate all day is no guarantee of spirituality. This is one of many false concepts about what it means to be "Holy." It is actually more challenging, and ultimately more rewarding, to embrace and live life to the fullest, all the while recognizing it as a gift from God. Being able to keep your focus while walking this gentle balance is indeed "spiritual."

Before I began to really absorb the teachings of God at Guidance for a Better Life, I lived under the illusion that the spiritual life was separate in many ways from one's daily physical life. My mind contained images of Christian saints, holy men from Asia, and other types of seekers, all of whom were in pursuit of spiritual truth. As I imagined it, they were ones who lived spiritual lives that did not involve being a part of everyday society with its careers, bills to pay, houses to maintain, and life amid family and friends. I did not understand at the time the degree to which living a balanced life, that allows one to function within the fabric of modern society, can be an integral part of traveling the path home to the Heart of God. I had a t-shirt that I had bought at Guidance for a Better Life that contained a quote from Del Hall, the Prophet, "Live in balance and harmony." I had not, however, truly contemplated what it takes to walk through life in this way.

Many years after my first retreat with Del, I followed a nudge from Divine Spirit to open up one of my journals in which I had recorded experiences from ten years earlier. As a result of following the nudge, I received more clarity as to how God has been communicating to me about living a balanced, abundant life for quite a while, as He helps me to create a life that works for me. In this journal I discovered a record of having seen green spiritual light flash in front of me. This occurred as I was reflecting on a dream that morning in which I had enjoyed speaking in a mixture of Spanish and English with a friend who was from Latin America. I also discovered that in a following dream from that same morning, I had spoken with a lady who looked rather like the friend in the prior dream, and that she had talked with me about my getting certified to do something that involved television, computers, or similar electronic devices. I awoke from that second dream with a feeling about a teaching career that I had been contemplating and how I needed to study Spanish more. At the time that I had been given the dream by the Prophet, I was not very confident in my ability to use electronic technology, especially computers. I was also more attached than I had realized to my manual labor job, one in which I would sometimes speak in Spanish with other workers. As far as leaving this outdoor job for teaching in a classroom was concerned, history was a subject that I felt confident in my ability to teach.

As I read about the green Light of God and these dreams in my journal, the message was now crystal clear. God and His Prophet want me to be happy in my daily life. This includes being happy with a career that I enjoy, and one that gives me many of the lessons of living that I need in order to draw closer to God. I remembered how Del has taught his students that green spiritual light is a form that the Light of God takes when there is a spiritual message for us that relates to something in the physical world.

At the time that I discovered this account of having seen the green Light of God, I was faced with the opportunity to make a career change from the familiar routine of landscaping and substitute teaching to that of working as a Spanish language teacher at a school that had offered me a full-time position. It had been a dream of mine for years to be a history teacher, but as I revisited my experience with the Light of God it was clear to me that the Divine had better plans for me, ones that involved teaching a language that I love. I was filled with gratitude in that moment to realize that many years ago God had planted the seeds of a new life direction within my consciousness. I also appreciated the clarity of Soul that remembering my experience with the green Light of God gave me. It was now clearer than ever that God was leading me towards a new career and that it had been a part of my spiritual syllabus for years to head in this direction, even though I had not been aware of it much of the time. To become aware of one's own true nature and God's plan for your life is a true blessing.

Right about the time I was blessed with this

gift of clarity I was granted another unexpected blessing, it came from following the direction the light was leading me in. Shortly after finishing my licensing exam for teaching Spanish, my heart was filled with gratitude for the teachings of Jesus. This took place as I reflected on the beautiful works of Spanish art and architecture that were inspired by love for him, ones that I had learned about in preparation for the exam. This gratitude opened the door to a beautiful moment on the drive home from the testing center when my heart was filled with an abundance of love. Love for Jesus, love for the Spanish language, architecture, art, and love for today's Prophet who had been guiding me every step of the way. Here I was, driving seventy miles per hour along a highway, my mind having been stretched way out of its comfort zone as I took a test for hours in a language that I am still learning, and I was experiencing the abundance Jesus speaks of in John 10:10! It has since then occurred to me that maybe the Prophet had guided me to teach Spanish, in part, so that I could have more true love and appreciation for this great Prophet of the past whose love is still with me today. God, through His Prophets, has always led me towards a life with more love in my heart.

As I write this story, I am now engaged in a new career that is giving me many lessons and experiences in life that I need in order to draw closer to God. I am blessed with many opportunities to think about the needs of others more than my own. I trust the inner guidance of the Prophet moment to moment while I teach my students and use electronic tools, such as computers, that are like those I saw in the dream ten years ago. What other blessings might there be in life yet to be fully recognized, if I took more time to contemplate what I have been blessed with over the years? What blessings do we all have hidden somewhere in our memories or in an old journal that has not been opened for years, waiting to be appreciated once we take the time to remember and look for them? I appreciate that God loves us enough to lead us into new directions in life that are tailor-made for us to grow closer to Him and His ways. Thank you God for the gift of your guidance. It comes through your Light and through your Prophet who shares your Light with the world. There is an abundant life that awaits all who follow his guidance.

Written by Roland Vonder Muhll

31

Healing of Anger

There are certain inner ills, like anger, we cannot rid ourselves of no matter how much we might try. It is important to do our part to tune in spiritually, such as singing HU, and ask for help from the Divine. By raising ourselves up spiritually we become more receptive to the healing.

My wife and I were separated and had been waiting for our divorce to be final when both of us were invited to attend a retreat at Guidance for a Better Life. It was a weeklong retreat and by the end of the second day unresolved issues between us were taking its toll. The third morning I got up early and took my coffee outside to watch the sunrise. I began to sing HU, a love song to God. The peacefulness of the sunrise began to fade as the darkness that had followed me here to the retreat center had its grip on me. I did not know what to do so I asked God for help in a very intense way. Almost immediately my body started to shake and twitch and I also started to cough incessantly, so hard that I had to bend over. As I was coughing I had a sense of something being expelled out of my mouth. A darkness came out of me that was like poison, not only for my body but my whole life as well.

After I calmed down I suddenly stood upright and felt as if the weight of the world had been taken off of my shoulders. I was so grateful for the amazing healing I had just received that I asked God, "What can I do for You?" To my surprise I received an immediate response in the form of a downloaded message. God just asked me to make amends with my wife. I was beside myself with what had just transpired but was so excited to share the experience; I thought I was going to burst before I had a chance to tell anyone about it. So when class started that third morning I asked Del, my spiritual teacher, if I could share my experience. After I shared what had happened that morning I proceeded to make amends with my wife. As I made amends the rest of the group began to sing HU very softly. What followed next was a feeling of peace so intense you could cut it with a knife.

Del confirmed that I did receive a healing that morning. Since this retreat till now, I have learned that anger is an inner ill and can only be healed by a true Prophet of God. Del Hall is such a Prophet and he helped me work through the anger I had brought to class that I was not even aware of. Singing HU that morning helped raise me up and bring me into a more receptive state so that I could hear the Divine message God was trying to get across to me.

I am grateful that Del introduced me to the HU song at an earlier retreat that I had taken at Guidance for a Better Life. Since then, singing HU has brought more abundance into my life than I could have ever imagined possible. Four months later my wife and I had the most peaceful divorce ever.

Written by Sam Spitale

32

As Soul I Remembered the Sound

Our journey through the Heavenly Worlds, our experiences with the Light and Love of God, and our spiritual growth will continue on forever. In a very real sense, there is no "finish line." Most of us however can point to an experience or a time in this life when Soul was stirred. A time when we knew without a doubt there is more.

It was one of my early visits to Guidance for a Better Life for a spiritual retreat. I did not know what to expect, but God knew what I needed and led me to that retreat. I am so grateful for the Divine guidance.

I first heard *it* as the weekend began. We were sitting in the field as a group singing HU with the Prophet. It was the beautiful sound of a flute. I have always loved that sweet angelic music, but this specific sound was so much more.

It was not the physical sound of any instrument I had ever heard. It was a beautiful and distinct spiritual sound flowing through everything. I was drawn to follow this flute-like sound as if I remembered it from long ago. As Soul, I recognized that sound was coming from God and was not a physical sound. It filled me with love. I was comforted and at peace with a sense of being more complete than ever before. As my physical body sat in the field I was free to spiritually soar with the Prophet. In what seemed like an instant we were in a place where I unknowingly longed to be and experienced a freedom like no other. Later I learned the flute-like sound is found on the fifth Heaven. As Soul I was familiar with this place.

The next day we were blessed with an offer to be taken spiritually to one of God's Temples. These temples are located in the Heavens. I accepted the opportunity and was led by the Prophet to a beautiful Heavenly space unlike anything I had a reference for in the physical world. It immediately felt so much more real than anything I knew in my everyday life with a heightened level of crispness and clarity. As I stepped forward I heard that now familiar spiritual sound of the flute, and it was again so beautiful and full of God's Love. It carried me in comfort and peace. Looking up my vision was filled with light emanating from what I could only describe as something looking like a castle. I went inside with the Prophet showing me the way.

We stepped into a large rotunda and I saw a huge beam of amazing, pure-white light flowing up and down. This active, sparkling beam of God's Light felt alive and nourishing as it illuminated the room and beyond. I recognized on some level that this was a very significant experience. I walked forward and put my hand up toward the beam as I looked to the Prophet to see if I had permission for this sacred act. With his affirmation, I put my outstretched hand forward and just let the light glide over my hand. There was so much in that light. It is God's Light and Love which I felt as peace, strength, love, comfort, and so much more. There were no words spoken, but this experience has had a lasting impact on me. I have had many more experiences over the years with God's Light and Sound, but in this life real change started with that intense and loving moment.

As Soul, I longed to reconnect with the Light and Sound of God. I wanted to let it flow through me as a child of God. The experiences that weekend gave me a reference. It started my foundation in this life to really know there is so much more. There is more than just this physical world. Visits to Heavens are possible. God truly loves us unconditionally. I could feel His Love in my experiences. There was so much more of God's blessings that I was not yet ready to accept, but they are there for me as I continue to grow stronger on my spiritual journey. I am thankful for these experiences and the continued inner and outer guidance of the Prophet.

Written by Michelle Hibshman

33

Grateful for God's Love

What better thing to be grateful for than God's Love? It comes in all shapes and sizes and it is personal. When we gratefully recognize it our hearts open more and we are again blessed. It is an upward spiral but the ball is in our court. When we appreciate the many blessings of God in our life abundance will flourish.

Yesterday Maria at work actually gave me half her water. I was trying to choke down the chlorinated fountain water and she filled my bottle with a purified cucumber and lemon concoction from home. I was at the spa with every sip.

We have not had hot water for a week and a half and I really appreciated the hot shower I got in the locker room at my job. It really struck me how fortunate I am to work somewhere that has a shower for its staff.

Then on the way home I was able to stop at my father's house. I dropped off some eggs from my chickens. Something I used to only dream about when we lived twelve hours apart. Dad and I talked through the screen in the fading twilight about our lives, God, and growth. I got in my car to go home and I heard the song lyrics "Ooh baby do you know what that's worth?... Heaven is a place on Earth."

Wow. I thought of a conversation I had at work with the family member of a patient. He was talking about racial conflict and getting along with coworkers. I said, "People see what they want to. Everybody has something good to bring to the table." This is also true with life. God's Love is EVERYWHERE. The package might look different, but the message is the same. We exist because God loves us.

It was in the water from Maria, the hot shower, the visit with my father, and even the song playing on the radio; each held a gift of love. Take a look around you today and see the love that has always been there for you.

Written by Carmen Snodgrass

34

You'll Kick Yourself

Soul is eternal and lives on forever but our physical life is short. If you see an opportunity for spiritual growth take advantage of it. Eighty, ninety, or maybe a hundred years for some, goes by in the blink of an eye. Make time to nurture your personal relationship with God. It's one of the few things you can take with you at the end of this life.

It was a beautiful wedding officiated by the Prophet, Del. My husband and I were guests, watching the young children who were there with their families dance with joy and abandon during the celebration after the ceremony. Del was well aware that my husband and I had recently learned a few social dances, and though we enjoyed dancing together, we were sitting out. After awhile Del came up to us and looked earnestly into my eyes and said, "Go ahead and dance. You'll kick yourselves later if you don't." I realized, "He is right!" We did dance and it was fun. There were no regrets later.

A few weeks after the wedding I began to hear this communication from the inner Prophet from time to time, "You'll kick yourself!" We had gone on a long weekend family vacation in Savannah, Georgia as a memorial to my husband's parents, who lived in Savannah for many years. On Saturday my husband and I, our two daughters, and their husbands drove to Tybee Island, the beach in Savannah. When we got there I wanted to run right down to the ocean and go in, not waiting another minute. But since it was still May I wondered what the water temperature would be, and besides everyone else was settling down in the sand for what I knew would be quite awhile. I thought maybe I should hang out with them. But I heard that inner voice, "You'll kick yourself!" I laughed, ran down to the water with joy and abandon, and went right in, cold or not. It turned out to be the perfect temperature to stay in for a long time, and I did. Others slowly joined in one by one, until only one of our daughters still had not gone in the ocean. Her husband said she was going to skip it. I said to him, "Tell her if she doesn't come in she'll kick herself later!" He relayed the message. She did come down, go in and really enjoy playing in the ocean waves.

On Sunday we went to Skidaway Island where the grandparents' home had been and to the very swimming pool with water slides that our girls had enjoyed going to. They wanted to share with their new husbands some of the experiences they had as kids. The girls and I remembered the fun we had going down those water slides. Now we watched children having a ball climbing up the tall stairs and going down the fast slides. I said to the girls, "Go ahead and go. You'll kick yourselves later if you don't!" So they did and their husbands joined them, all going down the fast slides heartily again and again. I went down the one slide that was open to sunlight. The other slide was a completely enclosed tunnel and I heard from everyone that it was pitch dark in there. Not knowing when I would be plunged into the water kept me from going down that slide. It was nearly time to leave the pool and I expressed to one son-in-law that I kind of wished I had gone down the enclosed slide. He looked at me and said, "Go ahead, you'll kick yourself if you don't!" So I did - a few times! It was scary at first, but it was fun.

Those things were fun. They added closeness to family and God because everything in life is spiritual and a gift from God, but the higher meaning of the expression "You'll kick yourself" that I had originally heard from Del at Guidance for a Better Life years ago was in a context that could not be more important. "You'll kick yourself," he said knowingly to all of us, meaning if you do not draw nigh to God and spiritually nurture a relationship with the Prophet, no matter how busy you are in life, you will regret it someday. These are amazing historic times to grow spiritually. Especially since the Hand of God is extended, as in no other time, to all Souls through a personal relationship with God's Prophet. It is an individual's choice to consciously accept this offer and the individual's responsibility to nurture the relationship. Life seems so busy, but drawing nigh to God is what is important and what adds more abundance to everything in life. This is what those words really mean for me. I wish I could pass on the gaze from Del's eyes, the eyes of the Prophet of God, as he spoke them to me.

Whether it is daily prayer, listening after the prayer, reading scripture, gratitude for blessings, taking the time to attend and enjoy a retreat, being blessed by being in the presence of God's Prophet at a HU song is so worth it, and what is the downside? At the end of this lifetime if you have not accepted the invitation to draw nigh and nurture a relationship with the Divine, and through that relationship experience an even greater abundance for yourself and your dear loved ones, "You'll kick yourself!"

Written by Martha Stinson

35

A Gift of Personal Healing

*To head out alone without God is folly. However, to sit
back and wait for the Divine to live our lives for us is
just as misguided. We follow our hearts and make the
effort, doing our part, and God takes care of the
"heavy lifting." It is a team and the strong ask for help.*

Although I have had many great experiences
and opportunities, I have spent a great deal of
my adult life attempting to figure out what was
"normal" and why I was not comfortable being
me. My ideas about what it meant to be happy
and content were ambiguous at best.

Partial answers to many of my questions were
indeed found through reading various books in
the self-help category. In them I often found the
possible reasons why I carried certain emotional
baggage. Also, the material I read about
emotions gave a whole lot of advice about how
to rid one's self of inner ills that hold one
hostage. Quite insightful, but for me ineffectual

since I never remembered to use the advice. I later learned that inner ills such as anger, vanity, and lust can only be healed by the Divine.

The real revelations and deep-seated healing came once I started studying at Guidance for a Better Life. It was there where I was introduced to the Prophet of God, my Divine connection. In time I became aware that I could not do it on my own and that I needed to get beyond the inner ill of vanity and ask God, "Please help me help myself." I asked in earnest. The very deep stuff that surfaced for me to look at and discard, with the help of the Divine, was the beginning of the healing process. Making the choice to think correct thoughts, use self-control, and practice self-discipline became and remains to be, key in maintaining the emotional healing as well as a sense of balance. By doing my part moment to moment and letting Spirit do the rest, I now no longer carry guilt over past mistakes. I am less likely to over react to life events and praise be to God, I am finally learning more effective coping skills.

The miraculous sense of true inner peace and freedom that I possess is something that I am now, and will always be, eternally grateful for!

Written by Bernadette Spitale

36

The Healing Power of HU

HU is an ancient name for God that can be sung quietly or out loud as a love song to God. Singing HU raises you up and opens you up spiritually making you more receptive to receive God's Love and healing. Those that have been singing HU for many years in their daily contemplations know there is always more to experience and learn about HU.

The HU was shared with me about fourteen years ago by my aunt and uncle. The first time I sang it in a group, I wept. It awakened something inside of me. My heart was opening to express pure love to God and I now know that it was the eternal part of me, Soul, crying tears of joy. I cherish singing HU and have grown to sing it faithfully many times throughout the day. Each time I feel refreshed, more at peace, and more grateful. Sometimes as I sing I am aware of a blessing or an experience and sometimes I am not. Over the years I have received a lot of healing when singing HU.

This summer at a weeklong retreat at Guidance for a Better Life I experienced a profound healing while singing HU. During an opportunity to have alone time at the retreat I hiked to Vision Rock, sat down, and sang HU. I did not ask for a healing nor did I even know I needed one. I just prayed to give all my love to God and be receptive to whatever and however it came back. I invited Del, the Prophet, whom I trust immensely, to join me spiritually. We met in my inner vision and to my surprise we traveled in our Soul bodies above space and time into past and future lives. I had an amazing experience and a healing that penetrated into the past, present, and future all at once. I was shown all the areas of my lives where there had actually been love, but it had not been recognized. I was also shown God's Love flowing into areas that truly were devoid of love. It was both a retroactive and future-reaching healing. To say my past, present, and future received healing during an out of body experience might be much for some to accept, but nonetheless it is true. My spiritual guide, the Prophet, is authorized to do this and it was the singing of HU that opened me up to receive this blessing.

It is humbling and exciting to know that I cannot grasp the full measure of God's Love, Grace, and mercy, nor do I need to. This healing showed me that giving my love to God via singing HU came back to me a thousand times over. It is difficult to put words to this healing and what it means to me. It is changing my life for the better and even changing the lives of people around me.

The HU continues to reveal more to me as I grow in my ability to receive God's blessings. I may never comprehend its value completely, but my heart knows that no matter what I go through in life God's Love can open me to Divine blessings. I know it was the singing of HU that raised me up to a higher level where my spiritual guide could bless me. This blessing would not have been possible without the many years of conditioning my guide spent preparing me for that healing. Without the guide, singing HU alone could not have taken me on the journey of healing I experienced.

I learned from that experience that we all have wounds we may or may not be aware of from this life and even past lives. We all carry a burden equal to our measure. They affect the way we view the world, the choices we make, and our ability to give and receive love. My experience while singing HU gave me more compassion for others and myself. I have always appreciated HU, but now I understand more of its incredible healing power.

Written by Tash Canine

37

Pink Carnations

God expresses His Love for us everyday. Often this love goes unrecognized because God communicates in many different and often subtle ways. Once you become more fluent in the "Language of the Divine" you will recognize God's Love all around you.

My father's favorite flowers were pink carnations. He really loved them. When he passed away in September of 2012, my mother had made the decision to not have a funeral or make any announcements of his passing. One day he is in the hospital and then he is just gone.

Months later I was attending a spiritual retreat in November at Guidance for a Better Life. I had gone upstairs to use the restroom. There sitting on the sink vanity was a bouquet of beautiful pink carnations. I stood there for a bit and cried. I knew these flowers were a gift from God. It was God's way of letting me know that everything was fine with my dad. He is okay. These flowers brought relief, peace, joy, and comfort to my heart. God knew how much my heart was hurting and that I really missed my dad. This awake dream was a gift of love from God. Thank you God for your love and comfort.

Written by Rebecca Vettorel

38

To Soar Like an Eagle

*Whatever the endeavor might be, concepts and book
learning can only take you so far. In the case of trying
to more fully recognize and manifest your divinity, as
Soul — an eternal spiritual being, actually experiencing
the qualities of Soul does way more than merely talking
about them. Those with a living teacher who can help
facilitate experiencing the boundlessness of
Soul are most fortunate indeed.*

During a recent retreat at Guidance for a
Better Life my spiritual teacher Del provided us
an opportunity to experience more of our true
selves as Soul. As God's ordained Prophet he is
authorized to guide seekers on journeys to the
inner Heavens. He gently helps his students get
to know themselves as the Divine spiritual beings
that they are. On this particular day I was blessed
to experience the exhilarating freedom of being
unchained from the confines of the physical
body and its limitations.

Prophet began by asking us to think of something we were grateful for as a way of opening our hearts. I thought of my pet chickens and rabbits that bring joy and love to my life. This brought a big smile to my heart as we sang HU, a love song to God. He then invited us to follow him up through the top of the room we were in, pointing out that in the spiritual worlds walls and physical structures were not barriers to Soul, which is made of God's Light and Sound. I left my outer body sitting in the chair as I rose up to the ceiling with the Prophet in our light bodies. The roof of the building just seemed to melt away as we passed through without effort. Looking down I could see the pond, the retreat center, Del and Lynne's house, and its lights.

Prophet then suggested we think of our favorite bird and I immediately thought of an eagle. I found myself soaring high above the trees and mountains. My large eagle wings moving in deep, slow, strong motions that propelled me through the air. I maneuvered unencumbered by the limitations of my earth-suit or the laws of the physical world. I felt free! I was tasting my Divine nature and the boundlessness of Soul. My vision was excellent. I could see even the smallest of details on the ground and watched various critters scurry in the grasses below. As a way of reassuring us that we were still our individual selves even though we were out of the body, Prophet asked us to think of someone we loved. I thought of him, as our love connection is so precious and close to my heart.

Together we soared up the valley and I saw Vision Rock, an outcropping of large rocks on retreat center property that has a magnificent view. It is a special place to us students. I remembered sitting on those rocks watching birds soar by or hearing jet planes roaring overhead and wondering what that might feel like. Now I had an idea, but this experience was not just a joy ride to me. It was sacred and purposeful. It also had qualities of peace, calm, assuredness, and strength that came from somewhere deep within.

Just then, Prophet said, "Do not go too far, stay close to the property." I think he may have been talking to me. I was having such a great time savoring the freedom and exploring in this way that I may have gone a little farther than he wanted so I circled back and made sure I stayed close. When it was time to return from our adventure we were asked to gather as a group and circle the pond. I still recognized other students at the retreat even though they appeared as light. Once we were all there Prophet gently and carefully guided us back down into the building and into our earth-suits.

We are so much more than our physical bodies. We are Soul first that has a body. What a profound and life changing perspective! For those of us blessed with this experience or ones like it, this statement is not just a mental concept or even a belief. It is reality. The Prophet arranges these types of experiences for his students so that we may gain first-hand knowledge of the truth in this statement and activate the qualities of our true self. With Prophet in my heart and by my side, I soar as a spiritual eagle in this glorious reality that is Soul.

Written by Lorraine Fortier

39

Tractor Ride With Dad in Heaven

❦

You need not wait until the end of your earthly life to see your loved ones again. The Prophet can bring you together to visit with them in Heaven now, even while you are still living. What a blessing and opportunity for healing these moments can be.

When I was growing up my family was very involved in our local church. I would go to Sunday school, regular service, and other events that were held at the church. There was one particular time when I attended a funeral; it was my first time and I was about seven or eight years old. I noticed the family was very sad that a family member had passed away, and they felt that they would not see them again. The question I had in my heart at that time was will they ever see them again or will they only see them in Heaven? As a young boy I asked my mother if this was true; will a family only see their loved ones after they die - only in Heaven? My mother said yes, that would be the only time they could see them again. I really felt sad for the family thinking they would never see this person again until they go to Heaven.

Many years passed since that day. As I grew older many of my family members passed on and I would think about them and miss them. I often wondered if I would see them again in Heaven. I attended a retreat at Guidance for a Better Life and I was taught that dreams are real and dreams are one way that Divine Spirit talks to us. Del, a Prophet of God, taught us that dreams could be healing, and if we asked the Prophet, he could guide you in a dream.

Twenty years have passed since I first heard that dreams are real and you may be able to talk to or see a loved one that has passed in a dream. Since then both of my parents have passed on and I have seen them again in my dreams. The dreams I have had with them have been healing and have soothed my heart. I have missed my parents and seeing them again and other loved ones in dreams has given me the opportunity to know that they are okay; it has been a blessing from God.

My dad loved to work outside either in the garden or ride the tractor mowing grass. I would sit next to him on his old Farmall tractor while he plowed the garden or mowed the grass; it was one of my favorite things to do as a kid. I had a dream with my father a couple years after he passed that was healing. In the dream he was driving a tractor and he drove up to me with a big smile on his face. No words were said, but I could feel the love that was coming from him and I was so happy to see him. We took a ride around the yard a couple of times, and he dropped me off where we started. I was so happy I did not want it to end. This dream eased my heart and let me know that my dad was okay. I was able to see him again! He was wearing a white shirt with work pants and his favorite straw hat. I knew that he was okay and that he loved me, and he demonstrated that love by giving me a ride on the tractor in the dream.

Knowing that this dream was a blessing from God has given me peace with my father's passing, and I am grateful. Knowing that I could see my loved ones again in a dream also gives me peace in my heart. How I wish that I could tell that family at the funeral when I was a young boy they could also see their loved ones again in dreams if they asked the Prophet. I am grateful for this knowledge and to have experienced seeing my dad again. My question was answered; I could see my loved ones again.

Thank you Prophet!

Written by Golder O'Neill

40

Divine Whispers Bring Blessings

God sees and knows all — all that has passed and all that will come to be. He seeks to share some of this vision with His children when there is an opportunity to bless us. The key is learning how to recognize and follow those gentle whisperings — those nudges or seemingly random thoughts for what they are. They are gifts of love in the form of guidance.

I remember exactly where I was sitting when it happened. The idea came gently, as if carried by a soft breeze through an open window. I could go visit my mother. A seemingly random idea, but I wanted to consider it. You see I have learned from the Prophet that when I place attention on gentle nudges like this I may be able to appreciate something more. Something I had not been aware of. It could be a loving nudge from the Holy Spirit to help me have a much more abundant life.

My mother had been sick for a long time. She was in her eighties now and her kidneys were failing but her condition was stable. Nothing had changed as far as we knew. I had just visited only weeks ago. I live in Virginia and my mother lived with my younger brother and sister over nine hundred miles away in Florida. It really did not make sense to go now. About six months ago she had been discharged from the hospital to home hospice care. I had been able to be there. It was a bittersweet time. My brother, her real primary caregiver for years, my sister, and I were there as the nurse explained things and did a brief exam. Our mother was frightened and confused and we all just wanted to help her. The nurse's name was Maria and we liked her right away. She was right out of "central casting," except she was not acting. She really cared. You could see it in everything she did.

I would like to share with you just one of the amazing blessings that were given in this. Maria had a beautiful Spanish accent and my mother just happened to love the Spanish language. I think this connected her to a very happy time in her life. A long time ago she was a bright college student working on a master's degree in the Spanish language. Mom was to have several different nurses take care of her over the next months. It turned out that Maria was the one who admitted new patients, not one of the nurses assigned to regular care. It seemed unfortunate at the time, but it turned out to be very fortunate indeed.

So, back to the idea of a visit. The gentle nudge or thought was to come again over the next few days before I suggested the idea to my husband. My mother really loved my husband and she had not seen him for a while. We could have a nice visit. We could fly to Tampa, rent a car, and drive the rest of the way. This would take us over a really long and high bridge that spans Tampa Bay I had seen on a previous visit that I thought my husband would enjoy. We decided to go. There just happened to be a great inexpensive charter flight available with the perfect departure and arrival times. We got in late on a Friday. My brother had told us right before we left that everything was stable with mom. He then greeted us with the news that our mother had stopped eating and was becoming unresponsive.

She did not seem to be with us much that first evening, and she had not spoken except for a few words. But as we started to say goodnight, all of a sudden in a strong clear voice she said, "I love you all." This was a pretty stunning gift for all of us, but I thought it may have been an especially beautiful gift for my brother. Maybe a thank you for his long devotion and care.

Many amazing things continued to happen over the next few days. We were able to arrange for everything that would be needed to care for her and everyone, as the time of our mother's passing grew near. Everything just seemed to fall into place. It was as if we were being gently guided by God's Love, and that is what was happening. We called hospice to come check her and check us to make sure we were able to care for all her needs. Her regular nurse was on vacation and so you may have guessed, Maria came. She lovingly examined our mother and said that she seemed exceptionally peaceful. We asked if she might be better cared for in an actual hospice. Maria said that if Mom was someone in her own family she would not move her. She would keep her right there.

Our mother peacefully passed on a few days later. We needed to call hospice and let them know and then they would send her nurse. Her nurse was still on vacation, so Maria came. She checked our mother, and then we all sat, talked, cried, and were just generally very grateful for how blessed we had all been. But the blessings did not stop there. There was the calling of family and friends. It was amazing to see the solace that was given back and forth. We had one sister and our niece in Puerto Rico and our older brother in California. Everyone was able to come. We were all able to be together.

Everything just worked out, down to the flowers, the food, and the pictures, to who just happened to sit near each other to say something, or be able to touch someone at just the right time. Everything worked out beautifully. It was way beyond anything we could have done. It all was an example of what a loving God does. Oh, I almost forgot to tell you that months earlier I had prayed and asked the Prophet that if I could be of help, could I please be there at her passing. It all turned out in the end like it always does, if we have the eyes to see. This may sound too good to be true. It's not. It's what God, the Holy Spirit, and the Prophet do for us, usually unnoticed.

This is but a glimpse of some of the abundance that God brings into your life through your relationship with His Prophet. I hope you may take time to consider what more there may be for you. His hand is out, will you accept it?

Written by Pam Kisner

41

I Pledge Allegiance to the Lord

You are not alone nor are you forgotten. God has always had a place for you in His Hand. In this hand is everything your heart has ever desired. It is a place of comfort, love, and deep peace. Whether you are aware of it or not, you are in It now. Those who have consciously experienced being in God's Hand are most fortunate indeed and nurturing the memory of this blessing makes all the difference in life.

I was resting in the Hand of God. A blessing of great magnitude, all by the Grace and Love and mercy of the Lord. I had consciously been brought here before by the Prophet of our times, but this time something was different. I was clearer and my knowingness of what I was experiencing was deeper. What I was experiencing was not visual in nature, rather a knowingness, and a gift and blessing beyond measure. I had grown through the years I had been attending spiritual retreats at Guidance for a Better Life. Under the loving guidance and nurturing of my divinely inspired teacher, Prophet Del Hall, I was more receptive to the blessing that I was receiving.

The Hand of God is so safe, familiar, and comforting. This is where I have always been, but had long forgotten. And now by the Grace of God, the Prophet was helping me to see, to remember, and to be aware of this gift. Do you remember what it is like to rest in the Hand of God? After singing HU, a prayer of love to God, for quite some time, Del's voice led us into contemplation and now all was still and quiet. Physically my body was seated on a chair in our classroom, but inwardly I journeyed with my teacher into the Heavens. It may sound impossible, but as Soul we are free - not confined to the physical world. We can travel into the Heavens to receive insights and love, and then return to live a happier life. With God and a true Prophet of God, anything is possible.

In God's Hand I sensed the presence of my dear friends and fellow classmates, along with countless other beaming and bright Souls. Yet it was simultaneously personal and intimate, as though I was alone with the Lord and His

Prophet. A moment of being cradled in Divine Hands. Love and comfort were pouring into me, present in every fiber of this experience. I needed nothing. Everything I had ever wanted was present here and now. A deep peace and contentment overflowed in my heart as I was being held in love. I surrendered even more fully into the moment and the love that was available for me. I curled into the hand, savoring this moment and not wanting it to end. The spot where I was laying fit me so perfectly, as if a mold was made just for me. There is a place for you in God's Hand. The comfort of this realization reached deep into me. What worry need I have in the presence of this truth? Blessings and realizations continued to pour into me. I am cherished. I am Divine. I am a small part of His creation, yet still significant in His eyes. I am love. And importantly, I am loved beyond my wildest comprehension. The vastness of His Love for me, and for you, has no bounds. His Love is eternal, unfailing, and everlasting.

Slowly the hand beneath me lovingly began to rise. Love in motion. And then the Lord of all placed each of us into His Heart, as a cherished and loved part of His creation. In this moment I knew that the Lord was pledging His allegiance to us, and with all my heart and all that I am, I pledged my allegiance to the Lord. Tears of joy fell from my eyes. To experience the Love of God is a beautiful blessing for which I am grateful everyday.

The Prophet began to speak again, leading us back to the physical world which we had briefly left to return to our true home. Now back in my body, I was aware of the little aches and pains that come with having a physical body and stretched in my chair. Yet I, Soul, was still aware of God's Hand beneath me. I was still supported in love. God was still holding me in the palm of His Hand. As I arose, I was still walking in love. Many years have passed since that special day. Yet His Hand is still here.

My awareness of His Hand beneath me as I travel through life shifts day to day, but His Hand is there whether I feel it or not. A few years ago, in a time of tribulation when my child's health was uncertain and we were waiting at the hospital for results, His Hand was there holding us. Times when my heart has ached, I have remembered being held in His Love. During times of joy, watching our children laugh and play outside as the summer faded into fall, God's Hand is there. In the kitchen washing dishes, His

Hand is still there. Walking through life with God's loving support is part of His pledge to us. It is our awareness of it that influences the condition of our lives. God keeps His promises. And He has promised that He will not forsake nor abandon us. No matter what it looks like on the surface, God's Hand is underneath us and His Prophet is here with us. It is thanks to the Prophet and the eternal teachings that I know, live, and experience this truth daily.

This testimony is to declare that this truth is ultimately available for you to experience too. You do not have to die physically to consciously experience being held in the Hand of God. His living Prophet, Del Hall, the Comforter of our times, is stretching his hand out to you if you are reading this. This is a testimony to share that it is possible to accept the love that God has for you. A guide is always here to bring us home. God has not forgotten us. A beautiful life lived in the Hand of God. Thank you Prophet for showing me the truth of God's Word and for keeping your promise to me.

Written by Molly Comfort

42

God's Promise Fulfilled Lifetimes Later

Earth is never without a true Prophet of God to help
show us the way home. Once you connect with the
Prophet you will never again walk alone. The name,
face, and scope of their individual missions may change,
but at his core, the Prophet is the same eternal
presence. What a comfort to know that even with the
passing of lifetimes we will not be forgotten.

I was sitting in the soft sand, smoothing it and playing with it with my small hands. I was about two or three years old in another lifetime long ago. The people of our group were busying about doing their chores some were chatting with each other. A few were watching the leader of our group talking with another man who had just arrived.

I began to watch this man intently as he was standing on a small hill talking to our leader. There was something very special about him as light seemed to emanate from him. He had a staff in his right hand, a long grayish white beard, and his white cloak was gently flowing in the breeze. The hood of his cloak covered the top of his head to keep off the hot sun. I watched in awe, for he exuded love and his eyes were bright with love. He caught my eyes looking at him in awe and recognition. Somehow I knew that he was God's Prophet, though I did not have the words for it. I had seen those eyes before and I knew that he loved me. He walked towards me and he put his hand out to me as he came up to me. I put my small hand in his, and I knew that he was making a promise to me. As he walked on he put his hand gently on my head, and I could feel love flowing from him into me. I was transfixed and continued to watch him as he and our leader were sitting in the shade under a tent awning talking with each other. Somehow I knew that one day he would find me again.

It is now, in this lifetime, and you are in front of me holding out both of your hands to me. I put my hands in yours. The love in your eyes bore into mine, as I realize that they are the same eyes that I saw as a small child lifetimes ago. You have found me, though you have always been with me. You are God's Prophet; I know it with all of my being. You are the one that Jesus asked God to send, when he asked God to send us a Comforter after he was gone.

But God's Prophet is so much more than a Comforter. He has shown me the way to God and he has shown me that I am loved, and that I am a Divine child of God. The Prophet is my teacher, my protector, my healer, my redeemer, and so much more. He is with me always and will always be with me. Having an inner relationship with God's Prophet makes life so abundant and a joy to live.

God's Prophet is here for you too, dear reader. He is here for all of God's children, for God loves each and every one of us, no matter what. Let him into your heart, listen to his loving guidance, and know that you are loved.

Written by Diane Kempf

43

Past Life and Promise of Healing

The Light of God can manifest in many different colors. Sometimes the specific color will provide additional insight into the experience. For example, many times orange light will accompany physical healing or insights into a past life. In the following example the author experiences both.

One of the ways that we grow as students of the Prophet, Del Hall, is to take his teachings home, integrate them into our lives, and go deeper. After a weeklong retreat this summer I invited his inner presence to join me for a HU song and contemplation. I had a soft intent to gain more information from the retreat and help myself with recurring neck and shoulder pain.

It was a beautiful Sunday morning and I was on my deck admiring the vegetable garden. We had just started harvesting some of the vegetables. It always amazes me what can grow from a tiny seed. I was reminded of the many seeds of truth Del had planted within my consciousness over the years that now bear fruit. The birds and insects were singing and I decided to join them. I began to sing HU, a love song to God. My heart was full of gratitude for my upcoming wedding. Although I was happy my body was experiencing pain. I had tried numerous therapies for a few months, which brought temporary relief. This particular morning I remembered a spiritual exercise where we can ask our inner guide to bring God's healing orange Light to an area where we have illness or pain. I decided to do this during the quiet time after singing HU.

I had a strong awareness of the Prophet's inner presence with me. I became more tuned in to a sense that there was no separation between us. I was within the cosmic fabric that sustains everything. A strong reverence for the presence that encompassed me gave way to an orange effervescent light that cascaded over my being and into my physical body. It went to the source of pain, which unexpectedly became an impression of an arrow breaking through the left side of my upper shoulder from behind. This immediately sent a shooting nerve pain into my neck. It really hurt.

This was the recurring pain that I kept having off and on. Still deep in contemplation I remembered that orange light is also one way God can reveal past lives to us. There was a lot of orange light in my inner vision. A name from a past life and time period came to me. I knew that I was not this particular person from the past, but the clue was that I was alive during this time in history and had sustained a battle wound in this area of my body. I had a vision of breaking the wooden shaft off where the arrow came through. I pulled the weapon out of my flesh. There was a sense of an infection that set in many days later and no more was revealed to me.

After this contemplation the pain that was there subsided. It had been dulled through this experience as if God's Prophet put a soothing balm on it. I was given a knowing that I need to be patient with this healing. It had many layers and would not be in my best interest at this time to simply fix the pain and move on. There was more to come over the year and I would get it as I could accept it. This lifetime was thousands of years back. I suppose I should have been more surprised at this but I wasn't. Anything is possible with God's Prophet. I can testify that he will do just about anything to help us (with our permission) to accept more of God's Love and more of our own divinity. This is one of many occasions when I was given such grace.

I had been conditioned for this gift of love during the weeklong retreat I attended and frankly, over many lifetimes. Being taken back several thousand years was not random. The pain I was having wasn't random. It all ties into my personal journey over the years. There is a golden thread of love and truth that connects every experience I have and ever will have.

I was given a blessing with God's orange Light which brought insight into where my neck pain originated, temporary relief from the physical pain, and a knowingness that I am in the middle of a healing that is going to take more time to become permanent. It is a gift of love to be reassured of this, which brings greater trust throughout the process. I have come to learn that I have an easier time giving love than accepting it. With each healing from the past a greater ability to accept love has been given to me. The greatest joy I have found in life is the joy of giving. However, one can only give out what he or she can first accept.

I am so grateful to have learned some of the language of God. I know that many times colors of specific light are an expression of love, which contains infinite blessings.

Written by Tash Canine

44

God's Love Has Always Been With Me

The Prophet can allow us to spiritually revisit and relive experiences from our past to gain a higher understanding. These sacred opportunities can be very healing. In the following example it helps the author realize one of the most important truths, that she has always and will always be loved by God.

While at a retreat at Guidance for a Better Life I had some time to be alone and to contemplate. I was lying on my stomach in the grass looking down at the grass, like I used to do as a child. My thoughts drifted back to my earliest memory of when I was a baby in my crib. It was in the morning and I was sitting up playing happily. I have remembered this early memory for over fifty years. However this time it was very different. I relived the experience and I was intensely aware of God's Love all around me. It was very palatable. I felt loved, peace, and comfort. I was surrounded by love. My eyes were opened to what has been around me all of my life. God's Love has always been with me and always will be.

After that experience I have been seeing God's Love around me wherever I go. At home, at work, in town, and out in nature. I really truly know without a doubt that we are loved.

Later at that same retreat I remembered another childhood experience when I was older. In the memory I was lying in my bed at night during a thunderstorm. As a child I had always been afraid in the dark. That night, during a lightning flash, I saw a man standing in my room. Of course I was terrified. I screamed and my parents came in and turned on the light. Since then I came to recognize the man as the one who was the Prophet of God during that time. God always sends a Prophet to guide us, teach us, and lead us back home to Him - not just two thousand years ago. I did not know that then, and fear kept me from knowing the beauty of the experience.

At the next retreat during a long HU, I had the opportunity to relive that experience I had as a child. This time I saw it while God's Prophet of today was beside me and we watched the scene together. Love exuded from the man in my room, and all around me was filled with love just like my experience in my crib. God's Love and peace was all around me, but back then I was too fearful to see it.

I am so grateful to now have the eyes to see the love that has always been with me. God has filled my heart with love and pushed out fear, vanity, anger, and other things that get in the way of knowing His Love.

Thank you Lord for your love. Always.

Written by Diane Kempf

45

A Living Teacher

Singing HU tunes you in with Spirit. When sung properly it is a source of spiritual food for Soul by "raising you up" and "opening you up" to more directly experience the Kingdom of Heaven. The HU song is one of the greatest gifts God has given to Soul. Having a living teacher who can offer correction to help keep us on course is an even greater gift.

I earnestly tried on my own to know God in my life. I wanted to recognize His Presence and live a happy life. Into my early twenties I was an avid seeker. I tried different paths, meditation techniques, yoga, Sufi dancing - almost anything to quench the thirst I had inside for Spirit and for true peace. Yet all I found were dead-ends. An answer to a prayer led me to Del Hall and the Guidance for a Better Life retreat center. This is where I learned the importance of having a living teacher who fluently communicates with God and can teach me to recognize and understand my own communication with God.

It is a tremendous gift of love from God to have a living teacher and guide to show us the ways of the Divine. One reason that I have found this to be invaluable is for the correction we can receive from him. I experienced the importance of this first hand after having been a student of Del's for over twelve years.

I was using the tools and teachings Del had given me when I went through a time of hardship. I received an inner nudge from the Prophet to focus more on gratitude before singing HU to open my heart in appreciation. I followed his guidance and did this at home. Soon after, I attended a weeklong retreat at Guidance for a Better Life. Being a smaller, more intimate class, it was a chance to have more individual attention and focus more on the details of our journey.

HU is a beautiful love song to God, a vibration and prayer that can uplift us when we are afraid or need clarity. It is a cornerstone of the Prophet's teachings and I love to sing it throughout my day. It acts as a tuning fork that brings one into alignment with the Holy Spirit, but that winter my pitch was off. Instead of singing a pure HU, I was warbling. The effect was that I was not getting the spiritual nourishment nor upliftment that singing HU can bless us with.

Even the best instrument needs to be tuned regularly or it will be off.

In class Del pointed out that I needed to slow down and really sing love to God to be precise, not only in the tone, pitch, and volume with which I sang HU, but also in Its pronunciation. Without Del's seemingly minor correction, I would have gone on using this beautiful tool at home, but would not have had any lasting benefit in my daily life. I would have remained spiritually undernourished. This adjustment brought a real transformation in my quality time with the Divine. And as a result, my life began to transform.

Del once used an analogy of a ship crossing the ocean. A small error in direction would not affect a short journey, but for a longer journey a little misdirection means you end up on the wrong continent. There is a profound blessing in receiving correction from a living Prophet, precisely for this reason as we journey home to God. As a living student, we need a living teacher. One true blessing of having a relationship with the Prophet of our times is that he can give correction and guidance on the inner and on the outer as a teacher.

As it says in Proverbs, the Lord corrects those He loves. As an agent for God the Prophet gives truth, love, and guidance as well as correction to his students. At times the correction is in the gentlest manner and at other times it is more direct. But when the truth is accepted by the student, myself included, and the changes implemented into our lives - we see the fruits of the Spirit. Life is better when following the guidance of the Divine. Correction and pruning is part of an abundant life and our growth as Soul. Having a living teacher is a gift that I treasure to this day. His loving correction has truly helped me on my journey home to the Heart of God.

Written by Molly Comfort

46

One More Swim With My Dog

The friends, family, and pets we are blessed to share time with on our journey through life all have one thing in common. They help us open our hearts to love, which makes us more receptive to Divine love. In other words, the love we share with those in our daily life brings us closer to God. In the following story, "Man's best friend" is up to the task.

Paco and I found each other while I was living in Miami, Florida, attending graduate school. I was just walking in my neighborhood one day and this spunky golden dog with soft brown eyes pops out of nowhere and comes right up to me as I'm standing in the street. I let him follow me home and as the saying goes, "The rest was history." I was a daily runner and he became my running partner. Over the next fourteen years we would live in several different locations. Friends, relationships, and jobs would come and go, and he was there with me through all of it. One of our favorite things to do together was to swim in the ocean. He was a water dog through and through. Just the sight of a beach got him so excited, and I always loved the unbridled enthusiasm with which he would go bounding straight into the surf.

After a very full life that I can only imagine any dog would have been grateful to live, it was Paco's time to move on. Although I was very sad to lose my dear friend, I was also very comforted by the fact that I know Paco is soul, and that as soul he would continue on after he left his physical body. This rock solid knowledge that I had acquired through many years of retreats at Guidance for a Better Life got me through this challenging transition, and actually allowed me to keep peace in my heart. I felt and witnessed the Hand of God with him as he made his transition, knowing in my heart that he was going somewhere beautiful.

Less than a year after Paco passed away I had a vivid dream that I will never forget, in which we were swimming in the ocean together. It was a beautiful sunny day and we were in the clear blue water, doing what we loved to do best. We were out pretty far and at some point I decided to head back to the shore as I was starting to get tired. I beckoned for Paco to follow, but he did not want to come back. There was a mutual love and understanding exchanged between us, and instead of following me back to shore, he turned and continued swimming out into the ocean. I knew that as soul, no longer with the constraints of a physical body, he was letting me know he was happy and content where he was. And while I was given the gift of getting to spend some quality time with him, it was now time for me to return to my physical body and go "back to shore."

I had also wondered from time to time if Paco might be ready to reincarnate into a new physical body, as pets will sometimes come back to their same owners. I feel he may have also been letting me know he was not ready to come back. Whether or not I see him again in a physical body, I know that as soul he is alive and well. This dream confirmed that Paco did indeed go somewhere beautiful and is happy and doing great! I am so blessed to have been able to see my friend, swim with him again, and share real communication with him.

Knowing I am Soul, that others are Soul, that Heaven is real, and that our loved ones still exist after they pass away physically is a gift beyond measure. I am truly grateful to my teacher Del, the Prophet of our times, for this priceless knowledge of the Kingdom of Heaven.

Written by Laurence Elder

47

A Healing Banquet

Often the things that are causing us a lack of peace or holding us back have their origins in a prior lifetime. Our mind may not consciously remember the experiences but we still carry the hurt. When light is shined on the true root cause, healing can begin in earnest.

"Thou preparest a table before me in the presence of mine enemies" Psalm 23:5 KJV

God has the ability to bring us together in dreams to resolve the issues of the past, those that hinder our spiritual progress. I had the following dream while attending a retreat at Guidance for a Better Life.

I was at a large banquet. These were Souls I had incarnated with in a previous life. About forty to fifty people sat at a large oak banquet table filled with an abundance of food. Everyone appeared as they looked in their previous life. A comfortable familiarity existed between us, our love connections still continuing as if no time had passed. Other Souls began to arrive and join us at the table. Each of these individuals had caused harm to one or more Souls already seated. It was as if the verse from the 23rd Psalm came to life. The Lord had indeed prepared a table for me in the presence and company of my enemies. Yet they too were here for the truth. There was no preference for anyone injured over those who had caused harm. There were no victims here. All were simply God's children looking to heal so they could move forward spiritually in *this* life. This was an amazing opportunity to experience and witness. Truth and acceptance are a powerful combination. Forgiveness, of self and others, is often the byproduct.

I too had the opportunity to confront someone now seated beside me. Anger and unforgiveness welled up within me. Yet I was moved with deep compassion as I saw the openness and sincerity in this Soul's eyes. He genuinely wanted to understand what harm he might have caused. I pulled back my shirt to show him scars on my chest. These might have been literal scars from that lifetime or it may have been symbolic of the anger and unforgiveness I still carried from our encounter.

Suddenly I heard a soothing voice. I felt reassured and calmed as my body became immobilized. I felt safe and free to relive this familiar experience. Suffocating in my sleep was a recurring nightmare from my childhood. I would often yell and scream as I struggled for what felt like hours to wake. Yet I often woke to find my physical body completely relaxed and breathing normally. Now having been taken to the root cause, there was no longer any need to experience it further. I relived this one last time and by the healing Grace of God have been free of it ever since.

There is only so much room in our hearts. Del, the Prophet, has taught me that our choices and our responses decide in large part what we allow into it. Dreams are one way God can bring awareness to these matters and lead us to acceptance, which ultimately brings healing and freedom. This one experience has brought me greater peace in the form of more forgiveness, compassion, and freedom. I am grateful for this blessing!

Written by Chris Comfort

48

Invitation to God's Ocean of Love

❦

It is possible to spiritually return to our Heavenly Home, while still physically living, to experience God and His Light and Love. Those that have been blessed to make this journey with the Prophet know without a doubt they are Soul, an eternal child of God, and that God is real. They can now help God bring more light and love into this world.

I have been a student at Guidance for a Better Life for many years, and through those years I have been taught spiritual tools that have conditioned, uplifted, and healed me. It has been through my relationship with the Prophet that I have been very blessed to have many amazing spiritual experiences. I would like to share this one with you, the reader, now.

Several years ago during a spiritual retreat my teacher, God's Prophet, led us in a guided spiritual exercise. We started by singing HU, which is a pure prayer of sending God love. After singing HU for a while our group arrived on a beautiful beach as Soul, without our physical bodies. The Prophet and I were at the water's edge on our knees with our heads bowed. We were in front of an endless sparkling ocean of God's Love. My heart was full of love, appreciation, and reverence for being at the Home of God.

We were invited to look into the water and I immediately noticed a bright, live, brilliant ball of light - Soul. I recognized this as myself as Soul. I arrived at the beach in my Soul body but in this experience I was being invited to experience it in fuller consciousness. Every ounce of me wanted to experience the eternal me, Soul, unencumbered by the mind or the mind's filters. I went into this brilliant ball of Soul and I experienced love, joy, and fluidity; I felt light and truly alive - free. Soul is truly alive and is fluid in opposition to being rigid and weighed down, like we feel here in our physical bodies. As humans, learning how to operate as Soul is a most remarkable experience. We are Soul, which has a physical body.

The Prophet and I were then back on the beach reverently kneeling with our heads bowed. We were invited to look up at an aspect of God. I saw an infinite all encompassing brilliant light, there are no words to describe it, and within this light I saw the Face of God. If that wasn't enough we were invited into it and I went into the Light of God. I was engulfed with pure love through every fiber of my being. I was given a gift of a golden heart with "God" written on it, and I put this Divine gift in my heart to nurture, love, appreciate, and share. I had just received an amazing gift of God's Love that is still alive and giving. The magnitude of what I was being gifted to experience has no words, yet there was more.

We were back on the beach kneeling with our heads bowed. We were asked to take the smallest drop of ocean water and put it in our hand. I put my finger to the water and a drop adhered to my finger. I put this drop in the palm of my hand. The drop was alive and brilliant and within this smallest drop of God's ocean of Love was everything; it was complete. God said there is an abundance of His Love, but there is a distribution problem. He asked if we would like to take a piece of the ocean of love into the lower worlds of God and serve. As I heard and felt God's words my heart and everything that I am excitedly and fully answered, "YES." Then we were asked to put out our right arm and point our index finger outward towards God. God's Hand came towards mine and mine reaching towards His with everything in my being. God's Love, Light, and Sound entered into the tip of my finger moving and spreading through my arm filling all of me. I could see the brilliance and feel it as it entered into my finger traveling and filling me with God's Light and Sound. I accepted as much as I could and was told that this will grow with me as I grow spiritually. I was ordained as a servant of God to be an instrument for God and His Love here on Earth.

The magnitude of the experience fills me with incredible appreciation, love, joy, and humility. I can still experience the inner excitement of reaching towards God and God's reach towards me today, as I did then during the experience. Why me, one might ask? It is God's choice and I am in awe and humbled by it. It is through my relationship with God's Prophet that this and all things are possible.

Written by Renée Dinwiddie

49

River of Golden Love

Singing HU has many benefits for those that sing it. Ultimately though, it is not about us — it is a love song to God. It is a chance for us to give thanks for our blessings and express our love to God with no strings attached. God is a giver in nature so it is not surprising to realize He sends this love right back, to us and to others, in countless ways.

We were gathered with Prophet on a beautiful winter morning to sing HU, a love song to God. Over the years I have come to appreciate HU more and more. It has many facets and layers to what it is and what singing with a grateful, open heart can do. Learning about HU is like learning about God, it is never ending and amazing. Singing HU is a pure way to send love to God. It helps tune one in to Divine Spirit and open one's heart to receive blessings of love, peace, joy, clarity, strength, healing, spiritual truth, and more. HU can raise one up to a higher spiritual view to be more receptive to the Prophet's inner communication and teachings. It can also be a way of praying for others. It is not asking for anything specific or trying to direct God in anyway. Simply sing HU and send love to God with a gentle intent in your heart for others to be blessed, then surrender this prayer and let God take care of the rest. Our Father knows His children. He and His agent, the Prophet, know what people need and the best way to deliver the blessings.

We began to send love to God by singing HU. I had a conscious intent in my heart for God to use the love sent in my HU song to bless other Souls in whatever way He knew best. I then surrendered the outcome. I maintained my focus on sending love to God. Then a scene came into my inner vision. I saw a river of gold and was drawn toward it. I stood alongside this beautiful flowing river for a while then began walking upstream. I could see HUs arriving at the source of the river. They appeared as containers of all types that were filled with love. Some looked like coins, others as blocks or shapes of different kinds. As the individual containers were poured into the river they were turned into liquid gold.

I then followed the river back downstream through a valley surrounded by mountains. In the distance where the sun met the horizon, I saw the river pouring over the edge and down into a swirling vortex. I had a knowing that this golden river was a river of God's Love. It was being poured out from the Abode of God down to all the Heavens below. As God's Love initially went out, it was very intense and concentrated. I watched this from above and then experienced it from below as it came down into the lower Heavens. As it came into the lower material realms, below the fifth Heaven, it was toned down. And when God's Love came into the physical world it became even more subtle. It almost seemed that God's Love was being disguised in many ways so not to scare or startle anyone. It came as comfort to some, a smile to another, companionship to someone who was lonely, a warm meal to one who was hungry, a kind look, acceptance, and family. The delivery was so unobtrusive, gentle, or familiar that it was often not seen for what it was, a very personal gift of love from the Father to His beloved children. How beautiful it was to witness where our HUs go and how amazing it was to be shown some of what God does with love sent to Him when we sing HU.

In reflecting on this experience I have gained a new perspective of the blessings in my own life. God's Love is infinite. It is sometimes soft and warm as in this experience but it can also be more direct, intense, or seemingly disruptive. It may come as change in outer circumstances of life or through a life lesson that facilitates growth in some way. It may come by way of the Prophet showing truth about our self or a situation, or by providing an inner experience that brings a higher view of life. I am very grateful for the gift of love that gives me the eyes to see and brings deeper appreciation for the ways God expresses His Love.

Written by Lorraine Fortier

50

My Blue Bead

*It is a sacred honor and blessing to have the
opportunity to be taught by the Prophet of our time.
This statement is not coming from a place of ego, it just
is what it is — the truth. Not everyone will be taken on
as a student of the Prophet because not everyone is
ready to accept the level of God's Love and truth that
flow through him. For those that are, their potential for
spiritual growth is nearly limitless.*

Someone asked me recently if the retreat center I go to, Guidance for a Better Life, gives degrees or certificates. It struck me as an odd question at the time. How could one ever graduate from the spiritual nature of life? I wondered. All of life seems spiritual to me now. The question did get me to look at the retreat center, my teacher, and the teachings from a different viewpoint. I thought about how when one applies for college, he or she sends out applications in the hope that he or she will be accepted to learn at that institution. This person's question caused me to remember and re-appreciate the first time I was offered a blue bead from my teacher Del Hall, a true Prophet of God.

It was a Sunday morning in August 2005. A small group of students and I journeyed with the Prophet via spiritual travel the night before. I had been given the opportunity to meet spiritual Masters and Prophets at some of God's Temples of learning on the various planes of Heaven. I was beginning to awaken to these ancient teachings Del was bringing back into my consciousness. Everything felt so familiar, although I was a "new student." I felt like I was reunited with old friends. Sitting around a campfire, sharing meals, sharing the most intimate aspects of life seemed more natural than it should have. Somehow I knew that this was a safe place. These were trustworthy Souls.

This morning my teacher Del offered me my first blue bead. He made sure to explain that although the bead was just a bead, and we were not into idolatry, the bead was very special. I remember knowing that I would treasure this gift. The bead is a symbol to me of God's Love. It is a symbol of how many lifetimes I, as Soul, have wanted the opportunity to apply at this school.

To be accepted as a student of the Prophet of our times is not something to be taken lightly. It takes Soul many incarnations to become refined enough to be in the presence of a teacher like Del and to be teachable. Just as an infant would be wasting his or her time to apply for college without growing up and learning, so it is with Soul.

Although I accepted the bead back then and have appreciated each one I have been offered since, it is hitting me now as I write this, just how special that bead really is. Yes, on one level, it is just a bead. However, what is contained within those beads is priceless to me. I have several necklaces which have been made by hand with love and care by Del's wife Lynne. Throughout the day I find myself touching the beads. An instant knowing comes over me - I am Soul, a Divine spark of the Voice of God. The Prophet's inner presence is always with me. I am never alone. God loves me. I am most fortunate and grateful today and every day to be able to appreciate life, even on the hard days.

My bead reminds me that there is always a silver lining and to look for it. It reminds me to trust in God and to love God, love myself, and love my neighbor; to focus on love but not to be naive. To take responsibility for my life, to treasure the teachings I was taught, and to care for the new life that it has brought me. To be able to introduce someone to the Prophet and the teachings is a sacred honor.

When I see a new student being offered a blue bead from Del I remember when it was offered to me. I am flooded with reverence, not for the bead itself, but for what it represents. When someone accepts it, I am grateful because I know that not only will they be blessed for it, but so will many others.

Written by Tash Canine

Guidance for a Better Life
Our Story

~⚬~

My Father's Journey

God always has a living Prophet on Earth to teach His Ways and accomplish His will. My father, Del Hall III, is currently God's true Prophet fully raised up and ordained by God Himself. He was not always a Prophet, nor did he even know what a Prophet was, but God had a plan

Prophet Del Hall III

for him like He has for all of His children. Over many years through many life experiences, God had begun to prepare my father for his future assignment, mostly unbeknownst to him. Everything he experienced in his life from the joys to the sadness helped prepare him for his future role as Prophet.

My dad grew up in California and was a decent student but a better athlete. He received an appointment to the United States Naval Academy in Annapolis, Maryland where he later met my mother. They were married two days after he graduated and received his commission as an officer. After a short tour on a Navy ship deployed to Vietnam, he went to flight training school and became a Navy fighter pilot. While attending flight school in Pensacola, Florida he also earned a Master of Science Degree and had the first of his three children, a son. After flight school he was stationed in a fighter squadron on the East Coast, where he and my mom began investing in real estate, adding to their family with the birth of two daughters. Following this tour of duty he was assigned as a jet flight instructor in Texas, after which, his time in the Navy was finished. He was a natural pilot and loved his time in the sky, but it was time to move on.

So far in life he had no real concern for, or even thought much about God, religion, or spiritual matters in general. He lived life fully. He raised his family. He traveled. He invested and became an entrepreneur starting and growing highly successful businesses in diverse fields ranging from real estate to aerospace consulting. Years before however, a seed had been planted when God's eternal teachings were introduced to him in his late teens, and while it did not show outwardly, the truth in these teachings spoke to his heart. My dad might not have been giving much thought about God up to this point in his life, but God was definitely thinking about him and the future He had planned for him. Like an acorn destined to become a mighty oak, the seed that lay dormant in his heart would someday be stirred to life. Through all his life experiences, both "good" and "bad," God would be preparing him for his future role as His Prophet.

When God decided it was time, He called my dad to Him. He did this by shutting down the world of financial security my dad had built. Over a period of two years all of his businesses were wound down and dissolved. What seemed like security turned out to be an illusion. Financial success had not provided true security. He now had failed businesses and a failing marriage and was trying to fix things without God's help, principles, or guidance. As painful as this time in his life was, it was yet another step towards the glorious life of service awaiting my father. God was removing him from the world my dad had created and furthering him along his path to his future role as Prophet.

After his marriage ended and his businesses wound down, he started fresh by going out west to give flying lessons near Lake Mead, Nevada. While living in Nevada my dad was reintroduced to the eternal teachings of God he first learned of as a teenager twenty-three years earlier, and though they resonated with him at the time, his priorities were different back then. Now, his serious training could begin. He started having very clear experiences with the Holy Spirit and noticed there was a familiarity with these teachings and experiences. He embraced the long hours of instruction, which often lasted until sunrise, and was receptive to the personal spiritual experiences he was given. This began an intense period of study and desire for spiritual truth that continues to this day. Some of his most profound and meaningful experiences during this time were with past Prophets of old. They came to him spiritually in contemplations and dreams. He learned of their roles in history and how they were raised up and ordained by God directly. He began to realize they were training him but was not clear why. A few times his experiences led him to believe he was in training to be a future Prophet. However, that revelation made no sense to him because he felt he was an imperfect person who made mistakes and had failures. He thought of the past and current Prophets of God as perfected Souls, not imperfect like he felt he was. Why would God choose him for such a role? He did not feel qualified.

Besides being introduced to God's teachings while he was out west, my father was blessed to meet his current wife Lynne. Returning to the East Coast, my father and Lynne moved into a small cabin on land he had acquired before his businesses shut down. This was a major change in his life, but it felt deeply right within him. He began to remember a desire to live like this as a child; from early childhood my dad found clarity and peace in nature. He had forgotten about this until now, but God had not and made this dream a reality. In addition to being their home, these beautiful, three-hundred-plus acres of land in the Blue Ridge Mountains would eventually become the location for the Guidance for a Better Life retreat center. The perfection of my father's experiences from earlier in his life in real estate, providing the land for his next step in life, speaks to the perfection of God's plan. One of many many examples I could list.

For many years my dad took wilderness skills courses around the country. He specialized in the study of wild edible and medicinal plants, tracking, and awareness skills, and authored articles for publication. Inspired to help folks feel more comfortable in the outdoors, my dad and Lynne began the Nature Awareness School in 1990. Classes were focused on teaching awareness and the primitive living skills needed to enjoy the woods and survive in them if necessary. An amazing thing happened within those first few years though; students began to experience aspects of God in very personal and dramatic ways. Somewhat like my dad's experience out west, they found that stepping away from their daily routine and the hustle of life, if even for a few days, created space for Spirit to do Its work. Whether they were enjoying the beauty of the Virginia wilderness and tranquility of the school grounds or relaxing by the pond, he found students' hearts opened, and they became more receptive to the Divine Hand that is always reaching out to Its children.

More and more the discourse during wilderness classes shifted to the meanings of dreams, personal growth, finding balance in life, and experiences the students were having with the Voice of God in Its many forms. An increase of spiritual retreats was offered to fulfill the demand and over time became the predominant class offerings; the wilderness survival skills classes eventually fading away completely. The name "Nature Awareness School" seemed to be less fitting for what was actually being taught now and in February 2019 my father changed the name of the retreat center to Guidance for a Better Life.

Throughout this time my father's training and spiritual study continued. My father reached mastership and was ordained by God on July 7, 1999 but he was still not yet Prophet, more was required. On October 22, 2012, twenty-five years since his full-time intensive training had begun, God ordained him as His chosen Prophet, and He has continued to raise him up further since. God works through my father in very direct and beneficial ways for his students. Hundreds and hundreds of students for more than thirty years have received God's eternal teachings through my father's instruction and mentoring. They have had personal experiences with the Divine which have transformed and greatly blessed their lives. My father's greatest joy is being used by God as a servant to share God's ways and truths with thirsty Souls and hungry seekers. In addition to mountaintop retreats, my father continues to spread God's ways and teachings that so greatly blessed his life and the lives of his loved ones in many ways, including his books and videos.

Maybe you are at a turning point in your life and looking for direction. Maybe you have a knowing there is more to life but not sure what that might be or how to find it. Or, maybe you are simply drawn to what you read and hear in our stories. God speaks to our hearts and calls each of us in many different ways. Like my father's journey demonstrates, it doesn't matter where you started or the twists, turns, or seeming dead-ends your life has taken; God wants us to know Him more fully, and for us to know our purpose within His creation. He wants us to experience His Love regardless of our religious path or lack thereof. He always has a living Prophet here on Earth to help us accomplish His desire for us — to show us the way home to Him and to experience more abundance in our lives while we are still living here on Earth. God's Prophet today is my father, Del Hall III. You have the opportunity to grow spiritually through God's teachings which Prophet shares. His guidance for a better life is available for you — please accept it.

Written by Del Hall IV

My Son, Del Hall IV

My son, Del Hall IV, joined Guidance for a Better Life as an instructor after fifteen years of in-class training with me, his father. He helped develop the five-step Keys to Spiritual Freedom Study Program and facilitates the first two courses in the program: Step One "Tools to Recognize Divine Guidance" and Step Two "Understanding Divine Guidance." Del also teaches people about the rich history of dream study and how to better recall their own dreams during the Dream Study Workshops, which he hosts around the country. He is qualified to step in and facilitate any of my retreats should the need arise.

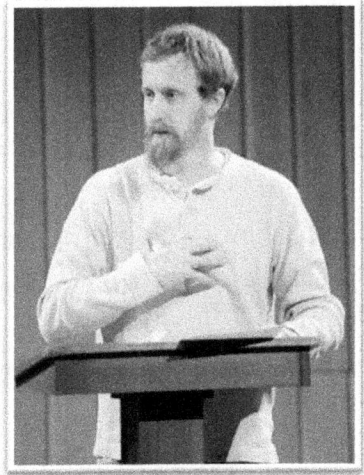

Del authored the book *God is in the Garden*, a priceless book of wisdom in the form of

Del Hall IV

parables. Through stories of everyday events of life on the mountain Del shares profound insights into the nature of God and life that are infused with his natural humor and unique perspective.

Del is also Vice President of Marketing and helps with everything required to get the "good news" from Guidance for a Better Life out to hungry seekers: everything from book publishing, blogging, and posting on social media outlets. He is co-author and book cover designer for many of our, thus far, twenty published books.

My son loves the opportunity to work on creative projects for Guidance for a Better Life. From a very early age he has been an artist and loved creating artwork in multiple mediums. He was accepted into gifted art programs in Virginia Beach, Virginia and then after high school graduation he attended the School of the Museum of Fine Arts in Boston. He is now a nationally exhibited artist and his *Paintings of the Light and Sound of God* are in over two hundred public and private collections. One of the greatest joys of the painting process for Del is using his paintings as an opportunity to share with others the inspiration behind them, God's

Love and his experiences with the Light and Sound of God, the Holy Spirit, in contemplation and in waking life.

Del lives on the retreat center property in the Blue Ridge Mountains of Virginia with his wife where they raised and homeschooled my three grandchildren. Recently he helped me with an extensive renovation and update for the three hand-built log cabins on retreat center property originally used for advanced spiritual retreats. He loves woodworking, tending to his vegetable garden, pruning his fruit trees, and helping maintain the beautiful three-hundred acres of retreat center property for students to enjoy. There is always something that needs attention on the land and Del is always up to the challenge. He loves to travel and spends his free time enjoying this beautiful country with his family in their RV.

My son has had multiple brain surgeries starting when he was seventeen years old for a recurring brain tumor. He credits God for surviving and thriving all this time when most with his condition do not. He looks to the sunrise every day with gratitude for yet another chance at life. With that chance he desires to help me share the love and teachings of God that have so blessed our lives. I pray to God daily thanking Him for my son's good health.

Written by Prophet Del Hall

What is the Role of God's Prophet?

An introductory understanding of God's handpicked and Divinely trained Prophet is necessary to fully benefit from reading this book. God ALWAYS has a living Prophet of His choice on Earth. He has a physical body with a limited number of students, but the inner spiritual side of Prophet is limitless. Spiritually he can help countless numbers of Souls all over the world, no matter what religion or path they are on — even if that is no path at all. He teaches the ways of God and shares the Light and Sound of God. He delivers the living Word of God. Prophet can teach you physically as well as through dreams, and he can lift you into the Heavens of God. He offers protection, peace, teachings, guidance, healing, and love.

Each of God's Prophets throughout history has a unique mission. One may only have a few students with the sole intent to keep God's teachings and truth alive. God may use another to change the course of history. God's Prophets are usually trained by both the current and former Prophets. The Prophet is tested and trained over a very long period of time. The earlier Prophets are physically gone but teach the new Prophet in the inner spiritual worlds. This serves two main purposes: the trainee becomes very adept at spiritual travel and gains wisdom from those in whose shoes he will someday walk. This is vital training because the Prophet is the one who must safely prepare and then take his students into the Heavens and back.

There are many levels of Heaven, also called planes or mansions. Saint Paul once claimed to know a man who went to the third Heaven. Actually it was Paul himself that went, but the pearl is, if there is a third Heaven, it presumes a first and second Heaven also exist. The first Heaven is often referred to as the Astral plane. Even on just that one plane of existence there are over one hundred sub-planes. This Heaven is where most people go after passing, unless they receive training while still here in their physical body. Without a guide who is trained properly in the ways of God a student could misunderstand the intended lesson and become confused as to what is truth. The inner worlds are enormous compared to the physical worlds. They are very real and can be explored safely when guided by God's Prophet.

Part of my mission is to share more of what is spiritually possible for you as a child of God. Few Souls know or understand that God's Prophet can safely guide God's children, while still alive physically, to their Heavenly Home. Taking a child of God into the Heavens is not the job of clergy. Clergy have a responsibility to pass on the teaching of their religion exactly as they were taught, not to add additional concepts or possibilities. If every clergy member taught their own personal belief system no religion could survive for long. Then the beautiful teachings of an earlier Prophet of God would be lost. Clergy can be creative in finding interesting and uplifting ways to share their teachings, but their job is to keep their religion intact. However, God sends His Prophets to build on the teachings of His past Prophets, to share God's Light and Love, to teach His language, and to guide Souls to their Heavenly Home.

There is ALWAYS MORE when it comes to God's teachings and truth. No one Prophet can teach ALL of God's ways. It may be that the audience of a particular time in history cannot absorb more wisdom. It could be due to a

Prophet's limited time to teach and limited time in a physical body on Earth. Ultimately, it is that there is ALWAYS MORE! Each of God's Prophets brings additional teachings and opportunities for ways to draw closer to God, building on the work and teachings of former Prophets. That is one reason why Prophets of the past ask God to send another; to comfort, teach, and continue to help God's children grow into greater abundance. Former Prophets continue to have great love for God's children and want to see them continue to grow in accepting more of God's Love. One never needs to stop loving or accepting help from a past Prophet in order to grow with the help of the current Prophet. All true Prophets of God work together and help one another to do God's work.

All the testimonies in this book were written by students at the Guidance for a Better Life retreat center. It is here that the nature of God, the Holy Spirit, and the nature of Soul are EXPERIENCED under the guidance of a true living Prophet of God. Guidance for a Better Life is NOT a religion, it is a retreat center. God and His Prophet are NOT disparaging of any religion of love. However, the more a path defines itself with its teachings, dogma, or tenets, the more "walls" it inadvertently creates between the seeker and God. Sometimes it even puts God into a smaller box. God does not fit in any box. Prophet is for all Souls and is purposely not officially aligned with any path, but shows respect to all.

YOU can truly have an ABUNDANT LIFE through a personal and loving relationship with God, the Holy Spirit, and God's ordained Prophet. This is my primary message to you. Having a closer relationship with the Divine requires understanding the "Language of the Divine." God expresses His Love to us, His children, in many different and sometimes very subtle ways. Often His Love goes unrecognized and unaccepted because His language is not well known. The testimonies in this book have shown you some of the ways in which God expresses His Love. It is my hope that in reading this book, you have begun to learn more of the "Language of the Divine." The stories spanned from very subtle Divine guidance to profound examples of experiencing God up close and very personal. After reading this book I hope you now know your relationship with God has the potential to be more profound, more personal, and more loving than any organized religion on Earth currently teaches.

If you wish to develop a relationship with God's Prophet, seek the inner side of Prophet, for he is spiritually already with you. Few are able to meet the current physical incarnation and most people do not need to meet Prophet physically. Gently sing HU for a few minutes and then sing "Prophet" with love in your heart and he will respond. It may take time to recognize his presence, but it will come. The Light and Love that flows through him is the same that has flowed through all of God's true Prophets.

A more abundant life awaits you,

Prophet Del Hall III

Articles of Faith

Written by Prophet Del Hall III

1. There is one true God who is still living and active in our lives. He is knowable and wants a relationship with each of His children. He is the same God Jesus called FATHER and is known by many names, including Heavenly Father, and the ancient names for God, HU, and Sugmad (Pronounced SOOG-mahd). God wants a loving, trusting, personal relationship with each of us, NOT one based upon fear or guilt.

2. The Holy Spirit is God's expression in all the worlds. It is in two parts, the Light and the Sound. It is through His Holy Spirit God communicates and delivers all His gifts: peace, clarity, love, joy, healings, correction, guidance, wisdom, comfort, truth, dreams, new revelations, and more.

3. God always has a chosen living Prophet to teach His ways, speak His Living Word, lift up Souls, and bring us closer to God. God's living Prophet is a concentrated aspect of the Holy Spirit, the Light and Sound, and is raised up and ordained by God directly. His Prophet is

empowered and authorized to share God's Light and Sound and to correct misunderstandings of His ways. There are two aspects of God's Prophet, an inner spiritual and outer physical Prophet. The inner Prophet can teach us through dreams, intuition, spiritual travel, inner communication, and his presence. The outer Prophet also teaches through his discourses, written word, and his presence. There is no separation between the inner and outer Prophet. Both inner and outer aspects of Prophet are concentrated aspects of the Holy Spirit. Prophet is always with us spiritually on the inner. Prophet points to and glorifies the Father.

4. God so loves the world and His children He has always had a long unbroken line of His chosen Prophets on Earth. They existed before Jesus and after Jesus. Jesus was God's Prophet and His actual SON. God's chosen Prophets are considered to be in the "role of God's son," though NOT literally His Son. Only Jesus was literally His Son. Prophets were sometimes called Paraclete. The Bible uses the word Comforter, but the original Greek word was Paraclete, which is more accurate. Paraclete implies an actual physical person who helps, counsels,

encourages, advocates, comforts, sets free, and more.

5. Our real and eternal self is called Soul. We are Soul; we do NOT "have" a Soul. As Soul we are literally an individualized piece of God's Holy Spirit, thereby divine in nature. As an individual and uniquely experienced Soul you have free will, intelligence, imagination, opinions, clear and continuous access to Divine guidance, and immortality. As Soul we have an innate and profound spiritual growth potential. Soul has the ability to travel the Heavens spiritually with Prophet to gain truth and wisdom and grow in love. Soul exists because God loves It.

6. We have one eternal life as Soul. However, Soul needs to incarnate many times into a physical body to learn and grow spiritually mature. Soul's long journey back home to God where It was first created encompasses many lifetimes. A loving God does not expect His children to learn His ways in a single lifetime.

7. Soul equals Soul, in that God loves all Souls equally and each Soul has the same innate qualities and potential. Soul is neither male nor female, any particular race, nationality, or age. When Soul comes into a physical body at birth, the physical body is male or female, a certain

race, a nationality, and has an age. All Souls are children of God. We do not have to earn God's Love; He loves us unconditionally.

8. Soul incarnates on Earth to grow in the ability to give and receive love and learn to live the way God wishes us to live. Because God loves us, His ways of living create abundant, happy, fulfilling lives. His beautiful ways of living are mostly HOW to live, and less on what NOT to do.

9. God is more interested in two Souls learning to love one another regardless of their sexual preference. God loves you just the way you are.

10. It is God's will that a negative power exists to help Soul grow spiritually through challenges and hardships, thereby strengthening and maturing Soul. We are never given a challenge greater than our ability to find a solution to or understand the necessary lesson, if we use our God-given creativity, make sufficient personal effort, and ask for and accept the help available from the Divine. Soul has the ability to rise above any obstacles with God's help.

11. We study the Bible as an authentic teaching tool of God's ways, in addition to books and discourses authored by a Prophet chosen by God. We know the original biblical writings are

sometimes misunderstood, for example, God loves each of us regardless of our errors and shortcomings. God's eternal abandonment or damnation is not true. He would never turn His back to us for eternity. (Isaiah 54:7-8 and 10, Lamentations 3:31-32, and Hebrews 13:5)

12. Karma is the way in which the Divine accounts for our actions, words, thoughts, and attitudes. One can create positive or negative karma. Karma is a blessing used to teach us responsibility.

13. A child is not born in sin, however, the child does have karma from former lives. Karma, God's accounting system, explains our birth circumstances better than the concept of sin.

14. A living Prophet, including Jesus, can remove karma and sin when necessary to help us get started or to grow on the path home to God. However, it is primarily our responsibility to live and grow in the ways of God, thereby not creating negative karma and sin.

15. There are four commandments of God in which we abide: First — Love God with all your heart, mind, and Soul; Second — Love your neighbor as yourself. The Third is, "Seek ye first the Kingdom of God, and His righteousness."

This means that it is primarily our responsibility to draw close to God, learn His ways, and strive to live the way God would like us to live. God's Prophet is sent to show His ways. Our purpose, the Fourth Commandment, is to become spiritually mature to be used by God to bless His children. Becoming a coworker with God through His Comforter is our primary purpose in life and the most rewarding attainment of Soul.

16. All Souls upon translation, death of the physical body, go to the higher worlds, called Heavens, planes, or mansions, regardless of their beliefs. The way they live life on Earth and the effort made to draw close to God impacts the area of Heaven they are to be sent. Those who purposely harm others (except in defense of self or others), themselves, or live against the ways of God go to unpleasant locations on the first Heaven; to a location where they can learn how to do better, as a gift of love. The first Heaven has a wide range of locations, from very very unpleasant and hellish, to wonderful and beautiful places to spend time with loved ones while learning and preparing for future incarnations. Those who draw close to a Prophet of God, including Jesus, receive special care. We know of twelve distinct Heavens, not one. The

primary Abode of the Heavenly Father is in the twelfth Heaven, known as the Ocean of Love and Mercy. We can visit God while we still live on Earth, if taken by His chosen Prophet and only as Soul, not in a physical body.

17. Prayer is sacred, personal exchange with God and is an extreme privilege. God hears every prayer from the heart whether or not we recognize a response. Singing an ancient name of God, HU, is our foundational prayer. It expresses love and gratitude to God and is unencumbered by words. Singing HU has the potential to raise us up in consciousness making us more receptive to God's Love, Light, and guiding Hand. After praying it is best to spend time listening to God. Prayer should never be rote or routine. We desire to trust God and to know His will for us, and then freely and joyfully surrender to His will rather than our own will. God's Prophet can teach us the "Language of the Divine" which will help us understand how God communicates with us and help us recognize God's Love in our lives.

18. It is our responsibility to stay spiritually nourished. When Soul is nourished and fortified It becomes activated, and we are more receptive and have clearer communication with the Divine.

When Jesus said, "Give us this day our daily bread," he meant daily spiritual nourishment, not physical bread. The Holy Spirit is nourishment for Soul. This can be received by singing HU, studying Scripture, praying, dream study, demonstrating gratitude for our blessings, being in a living Prophet's physical presence or in his inner presence, or listening to his words.

19. TRUTH has the power to improve every area of our lives, but only if understood, accepted, and integrated into our lives.

20. God and His Prophet guide us in our sleeping dreams and awake dreams as a gift of love. God's Prophet teaches how to understand both types of dreams. All areas of our lives may be blessed by the wisdom God offers each of us directly in dreams.

21. Gratitude is extremely important on the path of love. It is literally the secret of love. Developing an attitude of gratitude is necessary to becoming spiritually mature. Recognizing and being grateful for the blessings of God in our lives is vital to building a loving and trusting relationship with God and His chosen Prophet. A relationship with God's Prophet is THE KEY to everything good. This includes a more abundant

life filled with the Treasures of Heaven Jesus taught about in Matthew 6.

22. We are to be good stewards of our blessings. We recognize them as gifts of love from God and make the effort to have remembrance. Remembering our blessings helps to keep our hearts open to God and builds trust in God's Love for us.

23. We give others the respect and freedom to have their own beliefs, make their own choices, and live their lives as they wish. We expect the same in return.

24. The Love and blessings of God and His Prophet are available to all who are receptive. If one desires guidance and help from Prophet, ask from the heart and sing "Prophet." He will respond. One does not need to meet Prophet physically to receive help because he is a concentrated aspect of God's Holy Spirit, and is always with us. To be taught by Prophet in the physical is a sacred blessing. Much can be gained by reading or listening to the Heavenly Father's teachings being shared by Prophet.

25. We have a responsibility to do our part and let God and His Prophet do their part. This responsibility brings freedom. Our goal is to

remain spiritually nourished, live the ways of God, live in balance with a core peace, and serve God as a coworker through His Comforter. We pray to use our God-given free will in a way that our actions, thoughts, words, and attitudes testify and bear witness to the Glory and Love of God.

26. There is always more to learn and grow in God's ways and truth. One cannot remain the same spiritually. One must make the effort to move forward or risk falling backward. To grow in consciousness and love requires change. Spiritual wisdom gained during our earthly incarnations can be taken to the other worlds when we translate, and into future lifetimes, unlike our physical possessions that remain in the physical.

Contact Information

Guidance for a Better Life is a worldwide mentoring program provided by Prophet Del Hall III and his son Del Hall IV. Personal one-on-one mentoring at our retreat center is our premier offering and the most direct and effective way to grow spiritually. Spiritual tools, guided exercises, and in-depth discourses on the eternal teachings of God are provided to help one become more aware of and receptive to His Holy Spirit and the abundance that awaits. With this personally-tailored guidance one begins to more fully recognize God's Love daily in their lives, both the dramatic and the very subtle. Over time our mentoring reduces fear, worry, anxiety, lack of purpose, feelings of unworthiness, guilt, and confusion; replacing those negative aspects of life with an abundance of peace, clarity, joy, wisdom, love, and self-respect leading to a more personal relationship with God, more than most know is possible. We also offer our videos, and more than twenty inspirational and educational books.

Guidance for a Better Life
P.O. Box 219
Lyndhurst, Virginia 22952
(540) 377-6068
contact@guidanceforabetterlife.com
www.guidanceforabetterlife.com

"A Growing Testament to the Power of God's Love One Profound Book at a Time."

If you could only read one of Prophet Del Hall's books this is the one. It is full of Keys to unlock the treasures of Heaven and bring more of God's Love into your life.

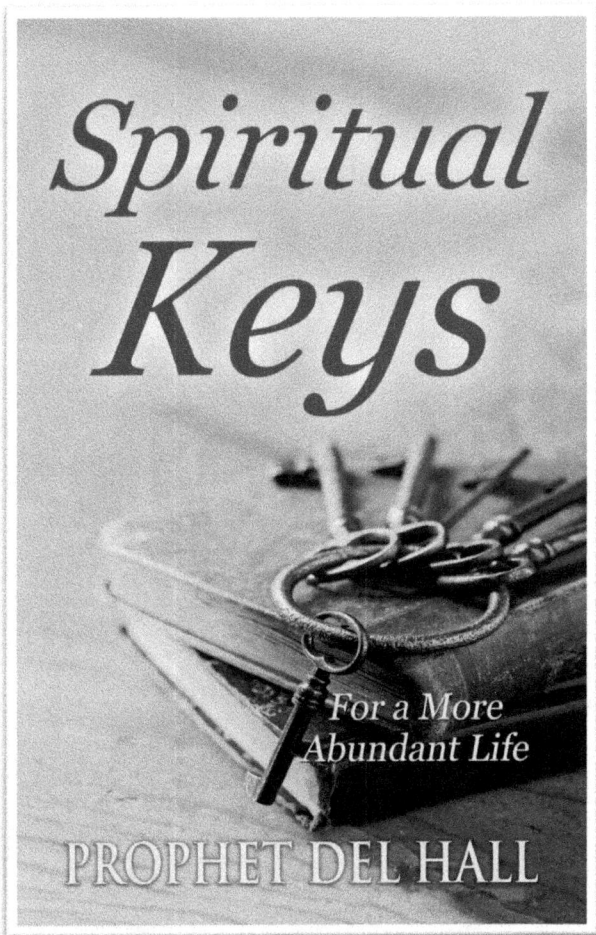

Spiritual
Keys

For a More
Abundant Life

PROPHET DEL HALL

Wayshowers are God's special emissaries to Earth. Our Heavenly Father loves us so much He has never left us alone without a Wayshower to teach us His true ways. This book explores the amazing history of God's chosen and ordained Wayshowers from thirty-five thousand years ago to today through specific examples of both well-known and little-known Wayshowers.

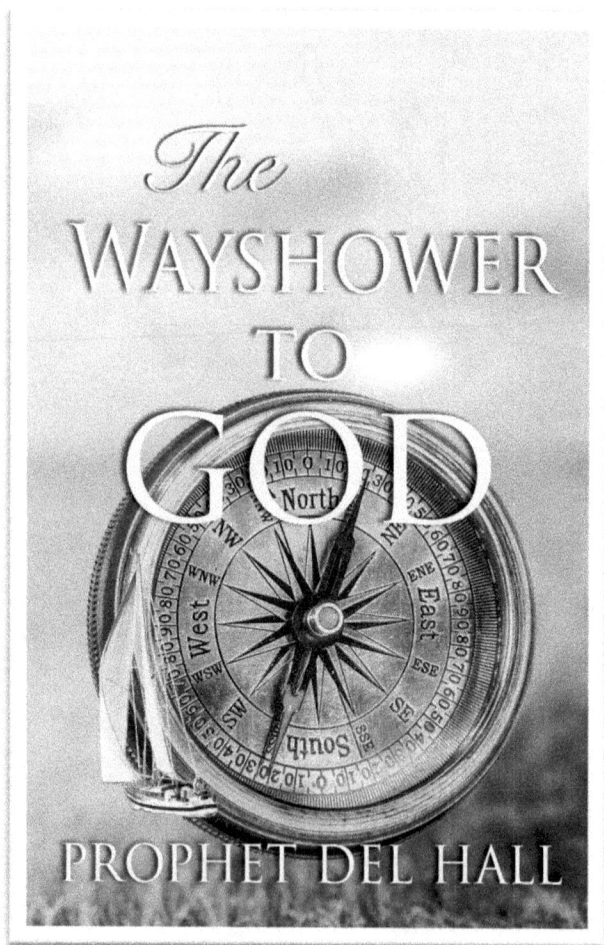

The
WAYSHOWER
TO
GOD

PROPHET DEL HALL

GOD IS IN THE GARDEN
PARABLES

Regardless of what your venture is in life you can benefit from this unassuming book. It may appear small, but the parables contained within have the power to affect your life in extraordinary ways.

GOD
IS IN THE
Garden

PARABLES
BY DEL HALL IV

ZOOM WITH PROPHET

Guidance for a Better Life retreat center has been hosting in-person mountaintop retreats at our beautiful location in the Blue Ridge Mountains of Virginia since 1990. When the pandemic began in 2020, it inspired us to get creative with how to connect with our students and new seekers. It was then our *Zoom With Prophet* meeting series was born. Some of these Zoom meetings are now being put into book form for those who could not attend.

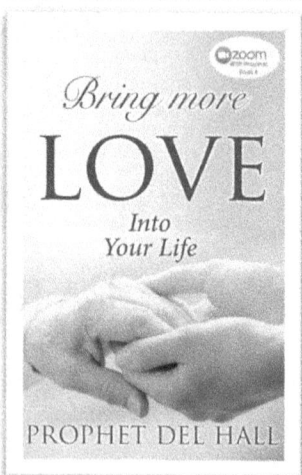

YOUR MAGNIFICENT ETERNAL SELF
PROPHET DEL HALL

BECOME Receptive to GOD'S LOVE
PROPHET DEL HALL

MEDITATION VERSUS Contemplation
Advantages & Differences
PROPHET DEL HALL

Bring more LOVE Into Your Life
PROPHET DEL HALL

SPECIALIZED TOPICS

Whether you wish to reconnect with a loved one who has passed, understand how you too can experience God's Light, improve your marriage, or learn how to understand your dreams, these incredible books have you covered.

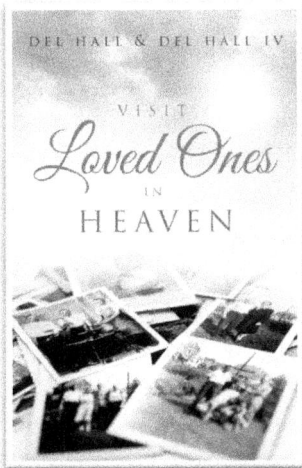

DEL HALL & DEL HALL IV

VISIT

Loved Ones

IN

HEAVEN

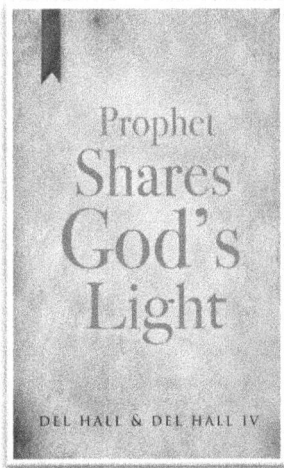

Prophet

Shares

God's

Light

DEL HALL & DEL HALL IV

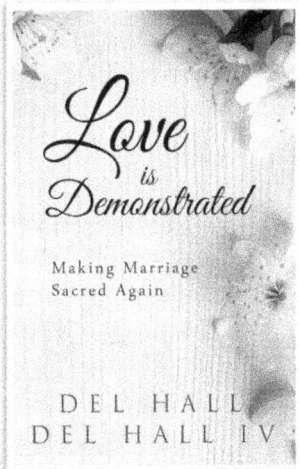

Love

is

Demonstrated

Making Marriage
Sacred Again

DEL HALL
DEL HALL IV

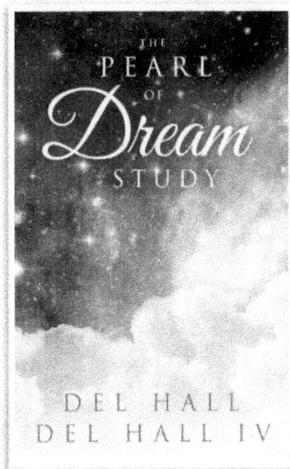

THE

PEARL

OF

Dream

STUDY

DEL HALL
DEL HALL IV

TESTIMONIES OF GOD'S LOVE SERIES

God expresses His Love every day in many different and sometimes subtle ways. Often this love goes unrecognized because the ways in which God communicates are not well known. Each of the books in this series contains fifty true stories that will help you learn to better recognize the Love of God in your life.

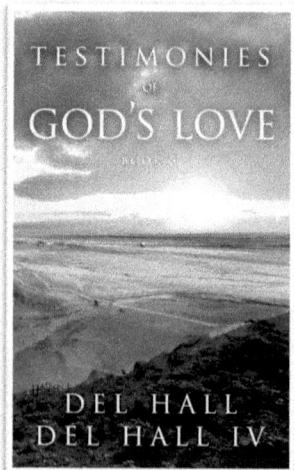

JOURNEY TO A TRUE SELF-IMAGE SERIES

This series includes intimate and unique stories that many readers will be able to personally identify with, enjoy, and learn from. They will help the reader transcend the false images people often carry about themselves — first and foremost that they are only their physical mind and body. The authors share their journeys of recognizing and coming to more fully accept their true self-image, that of Soul — an eternal child of God.